A PROMISE KEPT...

"This isn't just a how-to money book, it's MY story. It's intensely personal and a gift I promised I'd share with you while sitting on $5 plastic chairs that were part of the hand-me-down table I had in the "dining area" inside my 1974, 12 foot by 60 foot single wide trailer that I lived in for 6 years in the 1990's.

Back then, while I worried about my financial future, hoping someone would save me by offering me a dream job, I made myself this promise: "If I ever figure out a way to raise myself up financially, I'm going to share the solution with others that are in this same type of situation, hoping and praying just like I'm doing right now". It's been over 20 years since I made myself that promise, and I'm here for you now to make good on my words.

This Passive Income Stacking™ Handbook shows you what I learned to not only have the chance to move up from my mobile home days, but also be able to fire my regular day job back in 2004 forever. Inside I'll show you how to generate Passive Income so you're NOT trading your hours for a pay check, like with a regular "job". Plus we'll cover how to STACK multiple passive income sources so you have even more ways to potentially profit. Get ready to discover PASSIVE ways to CREATE money, and then PASSIVE ways to COMPOUND money. This type of SYNERGY is very POWERFUL! I'm hoping that what is contained in the pages that follow will provide you with a feeling of Hope, Enthusiasm, and Excitement about your financial future from this moment forward.

I'd also like to make you ONE MORE PROMISE now: I promise to provide you with NEW passive income sources to consider adding to your Stack, up and above what you'll find in this book, on a daily basis inside my **FREE "Extra Income Sources" online newsletter. As a FREE BONUS you will also receive the "Passive Income Stacking™ Quick Start Checklist" so you know how to begin with the most IMPACT! Please see what I have waiting for you now Absolutely Free... PassiveIncomeStacking.com/start-here**

I also promise to share more exciting details on money generating solutions with you on **"The Passive Income Stacking Show" podcast found here...**

PassiveIncomeStacking.com

Plus, I want to give you one more thing...

MY FREE ONLINE PASSIVE INCOME SCHOOL...

For years I've heard financial horror stories about the growing epidemic of student loan debt. People go to college in good faith with the hopeful expectation that they'll graduate with the ability to earn a nice income. Sadly, many come out of school realizing their income will be far less than expected. To add insult to injury, they're often strapped with tens of thousands of dollars in student loans that will stay with them for decades.

This schooling crisis frustrated me so much that instead of continuing to get upset for all the people being hurt by it, I created a FREE SOLUTION...

Centered around the Passive Income Stacking™ "money generating model" that you'll learn in this book, I created a FREE online school where I continue to teach online classes that cover even more strategies and insights designed to help you MAKE MONEY and reach financial freedom FASTER regardless of your age or situation.

Everyone gets a FULL RIDE SCHOLARSHIP to my Passive Income School where the tuition is FREE because YOU are the VIP! Let's start doing this together right now – first learn the strategies in this book and then take advantage of the Free Passive Income Classes TODAY at...

PassiveIncomeSchool.VIP

I hope this helps!

Mark~

WHAT PASSIVE INCOME GIANTS ARE SAYING ABOUT MARK WALTERS...

"I have known Mark Walters for many years and he's been extremely successful helping people create new passive income streams. If you're looking to generate more regular recurring monthly income then this is the book for you!

— **Than Merrill**, founder of FortuneBuilders.com
Star of A&E's "Flip This House"

"This book is a must read for anyone who is stuck in the life of work-earn-spend cycle without having much to show for. 98% of the world operates on just one source of income and wonder why they are not financially free. The financially independent and wealthy 2% have understood one thing, and that is that you need more than one source of income in your life. And ideally passive income. Mark shows you many options in this book and his "Extra Income Sources" newsletter. All you need to do is pick a couple and start taking action."

— **Jack Bosch**, "America's Foremost Expert in Land Investments"
www.LandProfitGenerator.com and www.ForeverCashBook.com

"Mark Walters has been showing smart people new ways to generate passive income for many years. He knows how ordinary people can generate extraordinary income, so they get more out of life! Mark's information is perfect for people who don't want to worry about money and who want to have healthy passive income, substantial savings and control over their financial destiny. If you want more income, less stress and a happier financial life Mark Walters is "the guy" you need to listen to!"

— **Robert Diamond**, Esquire, Attorney at Law
"America's Tax Sale and Overages Attorney"
www.TaxSaleBlueprint.com

"I've known Mark for years, we've had mutual clients and refer each other business. I wouldn't be working with Mark if he wasn't effectively helping supply our clients with unique and passive income sources to consider for a long time. He's helping people find new income streams, funding sources (Fund&Grow) and so much more so they can make more money these days.

— **Mike Banks**, Chief Operations Officer Fund&Grow
www.FundAndGrow.com

"I have been a multi-million dollar business owner since 1993. I have learned from my own personal experience as well as coaching thousands of others to success since 2005 that Massive Passive Income is best earned when you hire an expert coach and follow their lead. No need to re-invent the wheel and the "school of hard knocks" can be so much more expensive. Mark you have been a mentor to me for over 14 years. So happy you have decided to share your wisdom with others.

— **Tamera Aragon**, Lifestyle Freedom Trail Blazer
www.TameraAragon.com

"Mark has been sharing great ways for people to make money, that is extra money passively for decades. He offers a tremendous service and he helps people find new ways to generate income. He is the go to guy as he produces great information for all to benefit.

— **Ted Thomas**, America's Tax Lien Certificate & Tax Deed Authority
www.TedThomas.com

"Yet again, Mark Walters is helping entrepreneurs find true strategies to achieving passive wealth. This book will give you the resources, education, and wealth-generating tips necessary to becoming a success in any business!"

— **Lee Arnold**, CEO of Secured Investment Corp
www.SecuredInvestmentCorp.com

OTHER INCOME TRAININGS BY MARK WALTERS...

Passive Income Stacking™ FORMULA
Passive Income Stacking™ SYNERGY
Passive Income with Judgment Investing
Passive Income with Probate Property
Passive Income with Pre-Foreclosure Houses
How To Buy Nice Houses With Little Money
How To Manage Rental Houses For Cash Flow
Passive Income with Discounted Mortgages
The Debt Killer Method
And more found at...

PassiveIncomeStacking.com

"HOW TO REACH FINANCIAL FREEDOM FASTER
REGARDLESS OF YOUR AGE OR SITUATION"
MARK WALTERS

PassiveIncomeStacking.com

Cover Design by Printopya LLC
Interior Design by Printopya LLC
ISBN: 978-0-578-53017-8
Printed in the United States.

CONTENTS

PART 2 - Passive Income Stacking™ Sources

PART 3 - Passive Income Stacking™ Preparing For Success

INTRODUCTION

I remember sitting in my single wide mobile home back in the 1990's hoping and praying for an answer to my money worries. I had little in savings, very little money being generated, and a lot of concerns that haunted me on a regular basis.

At the same time, I hoped someone might understand and recognize my unique skills and abilities and offer me a dream job that would solve my money problems once and for all.

Can you relate with those feelings?

Needless to say, that never happened. And the reason is simple – most EVERYBODY who's in a situation like that, feeling a bit lost with few options (that they are aware of), is hoping for the same thing – that SOMEONE ELSE will come in like the cavalry and save them. The people that have figured out a money solution for themselves are usually looking to better *their situation*…not come and save others.

The good news is, for starters, you and I are both living at a time when it's relatively simple to create some extra money sources OURSELVES! To make this reality better, we have the chance to create these money sources *passively* (after putting in the work to establish and maintain them). And to make this scenario even better, we can outsource some of the work, when applicable and monetarily feasible, to virtual assistants. This can help free up our valuable time to consider MORE passive income sources to Stack.

While living in my mobile home decades ago, I had NO IDEA any of this was even a possibility for me. I learned this by STUDYING what money generating choices were available on a shoe-string budget.

I read all kinds of great books on money, from getting out of debt, creating budgets, compound interest, safer investment choices, dollar cost averaging, and simple monthly contributions to lay the foundation for eventual wealth creation.

In fact, you have most definitely already heard of some of the ideas and concepts in this book. I've seen a lot of them overlapped in the many books I've read and absorbed over the last several decades.

I'm a big fan of Dave Ramsey and his book, "The Total Money Makeover". I'm sure you've probably read that book, but if you haven't I HIGHLY recommend you do because you'll learn simple to follow strategies to get out of debt and grow your nest egg.

Tony Robbins' book, "Money Master The Game" is another terrific book that can help you, especially the insights he shares by interviewing many of the world's all-time greatest investors.

"Rich Dad Poor Dad" and "CASHFLOW Quadrant" by Robert Kiyosaki are two more great books that can help you a lot on your quest for financial freedom.

This "Passive Income Stacking™ Handbook" is a PERFECT companion to what you'll learn in the money books above, and many others, because it gives you yet one more "money-model" to implement to help you generate the necessary income you desire, yet in a PASSIVE way *without* trading your time for money like with a regular job. This is important because it helps you maximize your most important asset…TIME!

Of course you can have a second job to create some "right now money" if you need one, but this handbook goes into detail about another ADDITIONAL way you can be creating *ongoing* income *passively*.

Once retired, regardless of your age, you also don't want to be forced back into a job simply to pay for necessities. That isn't really being retired, right? But if you have even one passive income source, it can mean a lot for your security, peace of mind, and ongoing lifestyle. If you have MORE than one passive income source while you're still working or ultimately retirement, that can have a DRAMATIC IMPACT on your quality of life and FREEDOM.

The biggest tool we have to create financial freedom is our income, so what you're reading in this handbook is designed to create MORE income – without trading your time for money like with a traditional job. Regardless if you have one or two jobs, or you're currently retired looking for more income to live like a rock star, Passive Income Stacking™ gives you an ADDITIONAL income solution to consider.

If you're a busy person, stretched thin with overhead and responsibilities, this is going to be your SECRET WEAPON.

If you're an older person worried that you're running out of time to achieve a healthy savings, you're holding the answer.

If you're drowning in debt and need an additional solution besides getting a 2nd and 3rd job, this book has what you've been hoping and praying for!

I'm not claiming to have discovered something new. I have just taken what I've passionately studied all these years and positioned it in a way so that any one of us can climb into the CEO Position from the beginning on our quest of creating a mini-empire.

I was so grateful when I discovered this method was possible. Because like I said, nobody was knocking on my door when I was broke to give me a high paying job because they telepathically realized I was the perfect person for their organization. That's a dream…now it's time to create YOUR new financial reality!

What you're about to discover is something I've put together over a lot of trial and error. I've learned many of the hard in-the-trenches lessons, and continue to learn them and share them with my subscribers.

As I mentioned at the beginning, this isn't just a how-to money book, it's MY story. It's intensely personal and a gift I promised I'd share with you while sitting on $5 plastic chairs that were part of the hand-me-down table I had in the "dining area" inside my 1974, 12 foot by 60 foot single wide trailer that I lived in for 6 years.

Back then, while I worried about my future, hoping someone would save me by offering me a dream job, I made myself a promise. I said to myself, "If I ever figure out a way to raise myself up financially, I'm going to share the solution with others that are in this same type of situation, hoping and praying just like I'm doing right now".

It's been over 20 years since I made myself that promise…and I'm here now for you to make good on my words.

What you're about to learn inside this handbook should first give you a massive amount of HOPE! Next, it will hopefully give you the tools to begin your ascent, should you DECIDE to join me in this journey together. As you consider the solution that ultimately allowed me to fire my day job back in 2004, please share it with others so TOGETHER we can make good on my promise in an even bigger way. Thank you!

PART 1

PASSIVE INCOME STACKING™ ESSENTIALS

"WE NEED MORE CASH FLOW!"

Growing up my father would say two things to me about money that would ultimately shape how I earn income today…

1. "We need more cash flow."
2. "Don't be a one-trick pony."

I grew up in a family of entrepreneurs. My grandfather and father had their own businesses. So when my father would say "we need more cash flow", he was referring to the money that comes in on a daily basis.

For example, at different times throughout my life we would have some rental houses, but their positive cash flow was often minimal.

Other times we would sell a house to capitalize on the equity that had built up, but the profits would go into another investment that we wouldn't touch. Those investments were for long term wealth creation and not so much day to day living expenses. Because of that we often had less incoming cash flow than we would have liked. Can you relate with that feeling?

Because of this we were always on the lookout for NEW extra income sources. Some we found were better than others, and some didn't work at all.

Some would work well for a while, but then run their course and go away. We soon realized you can't count on one single incoming cash flow source. That's because you can become too dependent on that one source and then be left vulnerable to its existence. If it dries up, or gets reduced, you're left scrambling for a replacement.

When my father would say, "Don't be a one trick pony", what he meant was don't have only one way to generate income.

The combination of these two statements repeated to me over many years of my life by a man I admired greatly had a profound effect on me... and one I'm hoping can make a positive impact in your life as well.

The combined definition in my mind from these two statements was, "Establish many different ways to generate income that are unique to each other so you control your income and your life".

That made sense to me, but there was one ingredient that was missing from this equation when I was first starting out...

How was I going to find the time to uncover and generate all these different income sources?

For many years I had my father's words in my head, but I just didn't know how to fully realize them, until I discovered what would change my life forever...

PASSIVE income.

In the beginning I wasn't sure exactly what it was so I went to my father to talk about it. I asked, "Hey Dad, what can you tell me about passive income?"

His eyes lit up as he replied, "Well, I guess the day has finally come that you're starting to get this stuff."

That felt good to hear, but I wasn't exactly sure what "this stuff" was.

We always had a good relationship, and one filled with a lot of joking around. So he was having a little fun with me by saying, "Let me explain this by asking you a question. If you could have your cake and eat it too, would you be willing to work hard within a reasonable time frame to continue enjoying a great cake long after it was made?"

I wasn't exactly sure what he was getting at, but I love cake so I said "Yes!"

He said, "Okay, passive income is a way to make money without trading hours for dollars, like with a job."

I'd seen firsthand how much effort goes into working a job, so that sounded pretty good to me.

From that moment on I had a new vision of what money generation COULD look like. Now it was time to see exactly HOW I could make it a reality.

I have to tell you that I didn't know exactly where to find GOOD potential PASSIVE income sources when I first started. Like anything, this took me time to figure out. I made mistakes along the way, but that's how we learn, right?

What I'm happy to share with you is, I eventually started uncovering and collecting different income sources to the point where I'd get multiple checks coming in each month. That in itself was a MIRACLE to me!

Going forward I got out of debt, continued to fund my retirement, and in 2004 I fired my day job and have been doing what I call Passive Income Stacking™ ever since.

To be totally transparent, when I was younger it took me several years to "get my act together". I was working at jobs and not getting paid a lot.

From 1994 to 2000 I lived in this 20 year old single wide mobile home near the train tracks in an area of Phoenix, Arizona that wasn't considered the "good part of town".

It wasn't uncommon to hear gun shots at night. After each time this happened I'd look at my clock to see how long before you could hear police sirens - it was usually within 10 minutes, but sometimes there wouldn't be any to hear at all.

Just the same, I loved this mobile home! I referred to it as my "Mobile Estate". My folks kindly gave me some inheritance money from my grand-parents to buy it outright for $5,500. This helped me keep my expenses down while I tried to figure out how to best benefit with the passive income sources I found.

There's a shadow of me at the bottom of the photo as I took this picture of my favorite trailer back in the day. My *old-struggling-self* had no idea how much my life was about to change, and how much freedom and fun was just around the corner!

By the time I was finally able to fire my day job in 2004, I was 41 years young and ready to find more passive income sources!

NOW THAT YOU KNOW THE BACK STORY...

You might be thinking to yourself, "Okay Mark...what exactly is Passive Income Stacking™ - why should I care - and what can it do for me?

Great question...I'm so happy you asked! Let's get started...

ONE JOB ONE PAYMENT +
ONE JOB MULTIPLE PAYMENTS

Would you like to have side-money coming in on a regular or semi-regular basis ON TOP of the money you generate by working your regular job?

If you answered YES, then you're obviously awake and paying attention…that's good because it means you're ready for this!

Let's quickly dissect the title "One Job One Payment + One Job Multiple Payments."

"One Job One Payment" is what we're all used to as it's the regular way people earn money. You have a job that pays you for the time you're present, or for a specific service. In order to get paid again, you will have to give more of your time or perform an additional service.

"One Job Multiple Payments" is Passive Income you work to set up once - that comes in on a regular or semi-regular basis on its own in an automated way. It's side-money you don't have to trade your hours for like with the "One Job One Payment" method.

If you've heard about "Passive Income" and you just don't know how to start creating some for yourself…you're in the right place!

On the surface, Passive Income Stacking™ is a way for you to accumulate "passive income sources" so you get paid in a number of different ways – WITHOUT trading your valuable hours for money like with a "traditional type of job".

By diversifying several of your passive income sources, you're setting your income up to have less risk should one source be reduced or go away altogether.

YOU CAN DO THIS REGARDLESS OF YOUR AGE OR SITUATION...

If you're young and just starting out and would like ways to generate income WITHOUT trading hours for money...Passive Income Stacking™ is for you!

If you're a college student or you've just graduated and you want to knock out your student loans faster...Passive Income Stacking™ is for you!

If you feel stuck in a job that doesn't pay you as much as you'd like to be making...Passive Income Stacking™ is for you!

If you lost your job and are scrambling for ways to create income... Passive Income Stacking™ is for you!

If your debt is growing like a Whale Shark at a seafood buffet...Passive Income Stacking™ is for you!

If you're a single mother or father trying to make ends meet... Passive Income Stacking™ is for you!

If you were in the military (THANK YOU FOR YOUR SERVICE!) and are trying to transition back into the general workforce...Passive Income Stacking™ is for you!

If you're older and concerned that you'll never be able to legitimately retire...Passive Income Stacking™ is for you!

If you're a Senior Citizen and worried about outliving your money supply...Passive Income Stacking™ is for you!

If you desperately need more money coming in but you're stretched so thin you couldn't possibly consider getting an additional "job"...Passive Income Stacking™ is for you!

If you're just trying to find an "Income Solution" so you can realistically have a nice lifestyle that has the chance of getting even better... Passive Income Stacking™ is for you!

And finally, if you'd like ways to bring in extra income WITHOUT trading hours for money...Passive Income Stacking™ is for you!

Now that we've established that Passive Income Stacking™ may be a SOLUTION for you, are you ready to see how you can start benefiting with it as quickly as possible?

Yes?! Okay good! Let's Rock...

First, let's define what Passive Income is in the context of "Passive Income Stacking™"...

Passive income is income resulting from cash flow received on a regular or semi-regular basis, requiring "minimal effort" by the recipient to maintain it - after work has initially been put in to set up the income source to begin with.

Some income sources will require "more minimal effort" than others after the income source has been established.

In today's economy, there are many ways to create and maintain income that has the chance to be generated in an automated way. **Please realize though, it takes effort to create passive income to start.** This is NOT a get rich quick plan. I'm not making any earning claims here. There is no "free lunch"...everything worthwhile takes effort, right? Are we in agreement here? Good :-)

With that established, the fact that passive income has the chance to be generated on its own allows us to enjoy the income it produces while we're off doing other things.

That's important because having more than one source that generates income for you on a regular or semi-regular basis is what "Passive Income Stacking™" is all about!

That being said, please be aware you must monitor your incoming cash flow sources on an ongoing basis so they're maintained to keep producing to their highest level.

LET'S FOCUS ON YOUR INCOME

Do you have an income currently?

If you don't, then having a lot of potential "Passive" income sources to consider is like finding gold, right? Besides what you'll find in this book, you can also find currently added "side-money" sources on my website…

PassiveIncomeStacking.com/income-sources

If you do have an income stream, the odds are it's a traditional job or other means of income generation. Is the amount you're receiving each month from this one source of income enough to make you feel SECURE?

One simple way to measure this response is to determine if you have extra money at the end of the month, or *extra month* at the end of your money?

Do you have additional underlying debt such as credit cards, vehicle loans, medical bills, or student loans that never seem to get paid off?

Are these debts keeping you working harder and harder with no re-lief in sight - while keeping you from the lifestyle you'd much rather be living?

If you answered yes to experiencing any of these scenarios, the good news is ***THERE IS HOPE – AND A <u>LOT</u> OF IT!***

The challenge with having just one income source is that it leaves us VULNERABLE to the SOURCE itself. If the source should change or dry up, it leaves us unable to pay even the most basic bills for any extended period of time. That's especially true if we don't have much in savings.

One big problem with generating income the traditional way of "trading our time for money" is that there are only so many hours in a day and week to work and get paid.

So what can someone do to realistically generate more income when they're already stretched so thin with life's normal every day responsibilities?

That's when Passive Income Stacking™ can potentially come to the rescue.

The simplicity of Passive Income Stacking™ is to have <u>extra</u> income sources in place to add to what you're already making with your primary income.

I understand the challenge if you're already a busy person maxing out your time with work and life demands. How can you TRADE MORE HOURS YOU DON'T HAVE to make the extra money you might desperately need? That's an OLD mindset we can discard right now.

Please realize the concept we're about to focus on here is not merely "Income Stacking". To be clear, we're NOT talking about getting a second or third job that results in you getting stretched even thinner so you're exhausted all the time. That's not good for the longevity of your health, emotional well-being, or your valued relationships.

We're focusing on the VALUE and POWER of <u>Passive</u> Income Stacking™. That means income being generated that you're NOT trading your hourly time for a pay check to create.

Instead, you're setting up ways to get paid "in the background" of your normal daily life. This is money that's being generated while you're doing OTHER things.

It's "side-money" that's more AUTOMATED in nature.

Passive Income Stacking™ concentrates on potential income sources that can be set up to generate income for you ON THEIR OWN!

Yes, you'll need to spend some time evaluating each potential income source to see which ones resonate with the "Life Purpose" you'd like to create for yourself and your legacy. And yes, it will take some time and effort to initially set-up, monitor, and tweak these income sources going forward.

But once they're set up they're DESIGNED so they can continue running ON THEIR OWN, potentially supplying you with extra income each month for years to come!

THE POWER BEHIND
PASSIVE INCOME STACKING™

PASSIVE INCOME STACKING™
= CONTROL STACKING

Once you have your FIRST extra passive income source set up, you're in CONTROL of that money source. That's often more than can be said for one's primary income source which is their main job.

Should you ever get fired, or your position gets down-sized and your monthly income reduced from your main job, you at least have your first passive income source in place that YOU are in control of.

ALERT: PREPARE YOURSELF FOR AN OBVIOUS
"A-HA MOMENT"...

If ONE extra passive income source is good, TWO would be better, right? Of course…now we're getting somewhere!

That's the POWER of what I call, "Passive Income Stacking™"!

If having one extra passive income source gives you a certain level of CONTROL and SECURITY over your financial life…

By STACKING several passive income sources – you're also essentially stacking the level of Control and Security you have in your overall life as well! This can make ALL THE DIFFERENCE so you can pay your bills, get out of debt, and better prepare for the retirement level you truly desire and deserve…regardless of your age or situation!

That's why it's so important to scroll through my daily "Extra Income Sources" email newsletter – and listen to each of my Passive Income Stacking™ Podcast episodes. Both are free and ready to provide you with ongoing timely passive income sources to consider *STACKING*.

The resources that I enjoy sharing with you each day can save you a LOT of time as I've already done a lot of the initial filtering for you. But that's just scratching the surface with how Passive Income Stacking™ can help you "Time-Shape" your income…

PASSIVE INCOME STACKING™ = TIME STACKING

If you're older and concerned that time is running out for you to get control of your finances, Passive Income Stacking™ can help you get many of your "earning years" back as I will show you in a moment. (Because I started this later in life, this was a critically important aspect to me as well.)

If you're younger, Passive Income Stacking™ can help put you SEVERAL YEARS AHEAD OF YOUR PEERS – who often only focus on one primary income source.

TIME STACKING = MONTHLY/YEARLY INCOME STACKING

The math is so simple and basic that anyone can understand it…

For example, using some simple to follow Hypothetical Numbers, let's say you make $50,000 a year before taxes - trading hours for income (your job).

If you were to have just one extra PASSIVE income source on top of that - which could generate $50,000 per year, you'd essentially be doubling your income.

But it becomes even more DRAMATIC when you consider the <u>value</u> in terms of TIME…which is our greatest and most valuable asset after all.

Using the same hypothetical example – because you have these 2 income sources in place - you've reached $50,000 in annual income in HALF THE TIME! You're capturing the first $50,000 in just 6 MONTHS.

With only one income source (your job) you would have had to work a full year to make that amount of money.

Theoretically, by having the one extra passive income source PLUS your job, you wouldn't have to spend the *entire year* working and stressing to earn that FIRST $50,000 because you earned it in half the time (the first 6 months of the year).

Yes, you'll most likely continue working the following 6 months, but because of this ONE additional PASSIVE income source, you would earn an additional $50,000 annually for your extra effort of setting up and managing the one Passive Income Source.

When these 2 hypothetical income sources are combined, or rather STACKED, after one year they equal $100,000 in income.

Let me ask you this…

When you STACK your passive income and are able to DOUBLE what you make with your job – haven't you just captured a YEAR of your working life back? That's a year you WON'T have to work to make what your job pays you in one year.

Not only does that mean you can potentially make money FASTER…

If you're older, it also means you can CAPTURE BACK years of financial wealth creation that you may have thought were lost forever due to your age.

Or if you're younger, it means you'll work fewer years to become financially independent…which translates into doing what you want, when you want SOONER!

Let's continue our hypothetical example…

What if you were to have 2 extra Passive Income Sources that were generating $50,000 each year? When you combine them with your annual job salary – that's a combined income amount of $150,000 each year.

Think about it, it took you the same year to produce this extra amount – but only

4 MONTHS to generate your first $50,000!

So in ONE YEAR you were able to create the same amount of income that your primary income source (your job) would have taken you 3 years to generate.

This is a prime example of how Passive Income Stacking™ is also Time Stacking!

Obviously, the numbers in this hypothetical example are made up. I don't know how much your job pays you each year…or how much income each of your Passive Income Sources may provide you.

The point is, now you have a MODEL that can do POWERFUL things for your Finances, Freedom, and TIME left on this earth to make a better impact in the causes and lives of those that mean the most to you!

With your mind starting to open to the *hope-filled possibilities*, you can begin to dream a bit about the potential INCOME of some of the Passive Income Sources you ultimately decide to ACTIVATE.

With that empowering spirit in mind, let's continue our journey with how Passive Income Stacking™ might be able to actually help you pay your bills, get out of debt, and retire in style regardless of your age or situation…

PASSIVE INCOME STACKING™ = MONEY FOR DEBT STACKING

I have a course called, "The Debt Killer Method". It talks about how to systematically pay off your revolving debts such as credit cards, car loans, student loans, etc. Once they're paid, you then turn that outgoing payment machine on your house until it's paid off too.

That's fine in theory, but what if you don't have the extra income to be able to make those extra payments? Passive Income Stacking™ helps solve that problem.

Let's again hypothetically say you have enough Extra Passive Income Sources coming in each month to afford you $2,000 per month EXTRA to go toward paying off your debts such as credit cards, student loans, car loan, medical bills, etc.

You'll decide which one of these debts you want to pay off FIRST, while continuing to make the usual monthly payments on your other debts.

I've created a visual for myself when picturing how to set this up that I'd like to share with you in hopes it gives you a clearer vision of what I'm talking about. I call it, "Fire Hose Money™".

FIRE HOSE MONEY™

My internal vision of passive income is like having a fire hose, but instead of water, the hose is flowing out with money that you point in ONE DIRECTION. The direction is the ONE DEBT that you're trying to pay off first and FAST.

In other words, you're COMBINING a hypothetical $2,000 of Fire Hose Money with the monthly payment you usually make on the debt you want to get rid of first. Let's say the monthly amount you usually pay on the debt you've chosen to eliminate first is $200. Combined with the $2,000 Fire Hose Money, you would make a payment each month of $2,200.

As soon as that FIRST DEBT is paid off, you'll take the $2,000 in fire hose money, PLUS the monthly payment you usually made that went towards the first debt of $200, and you COMBINE it with the monthly payment of the NEXT DEBT you want to pay off.

Let's say the normal monthly payment you make on the next debt you want to pay off is $300. Now you're combining the $2,200 with the $300 resulting in $2,500 that you're paying EACH MONTH until the second debt is paid off.

You might be thinking, "where am I going to get an additional $2,500 a month?" Once you have that $2,000 additional Fire Hose Money™, you're simply combining it with money you already have that you're making your monthly debt payments with currently.

As soon as this growing flow of outgoing cash pays off all your debts – you may choose to point it in the direction of a HOUSE PAYMENT. At this point you'll hopefully have a pretty large "fire hose stream of money" that can pay off a house in record time.

Or, you might choose to point your Fire Hose Money™ toward investments like real estate, stocks, bonds, index funds, REITs, gold and silver, or anything else you like. (Always consult with your investment advisor before investing.)

Now, stop for just a moment and really try to imagine what having a source of money like this could do for you and your CURRENT situation.

You would FINALLY have a legitimate PLAN and MODEL to follow, to potentially EARN EXTRA INCOME PASSIVELY…

And then use this extra income to realistically and strategically pay off all your bills so you can finally get on solid financial footing again.

Once you're debt free – YES DEBT FREE - you can then turn your Passive Income Fire Hose Money in the direction of your investing nest egg to grow and compound. The more you put in, the FASTER your potential for wealth accumulation.

Like I said before, the math is pretty simple – use the extra money to reduce the amount of time it takes to get out of debt, create a potentially sizeable nest egg – and RETIRE IN STYLE.

The reality is this - if you *responsibly decide* to retire from your "day job" because you have your passive income stack kicking out enough regular income - that doesn't mean your Passive Income Stack™ stops generating income. You've only decided to eliminate the one income source that requires the most hours of your time and effort (your job).

PASSIVE INCOME STACKING™ = POWER STACKING

The more profitable Passive Income Sources you have to STACK – the faster you can make your dreams a reality.

You now know that the ADDITIONAL POWER behind Passive Income Stacking™ is what you do with your Fire Hose Money™!

Don't take it for granted and blow it on depreciating items. That's how so many lottery winners end up broke.

Instead, recognize it as the GIFT it is, and start to make TRANSFORMATIONAL changes in your life FOREVER.

If you have multiple areas that you'd like your Fire Hose Money™ to point to, you don't HAVE to point the flow of additional passive income in just one direction; you can spread it around if you like. That can also make it even more fun as you're providing a financial difference in more than one area that's important to you at the same time.

For example, you might put a portion each month towards your emergency fund, another towards your debt, another portion towards your investments such as real estate, stocks, Roth IRA or ROTH 401K, and another towards a vacation or car fund. Yes, you can have fun with this money too while you're getting yourself out of debt and into more wealth creation scenarios.

Life shouldn't be all about work and sacrifice. It's best to <u>reasonably</u> reward yourself along the way so you continue to have incentive to stay the course. By having a SMALL portion saved each month for fun things, it just makes the whole process that much more enjoyable.

PASSIVE INCOME STACKING™ = WEALTH STACKING

You've probably heard that when it comes to our income, we must pay our self first. That simply means a portion of our income needs to go into some kind of investment scenario. That could be real estate investing, stocks, precious metals, index funds, savings, etc.

The general guideline is to "pay yourself" a MINIMUM of 10% of your income each month FIRST, so you always have money being saved and invested for your future.

By having extra passive income sources coming in, you have the chance to pay yourself more than just 10%. You might have enough coming in to pay yourself 15%, or 20%, or 50%, or more. This gives you the chance to not only save more, but also potentially get that money situated so it has the chance to GROW and COMPOUND!

Depending on your age and financial freedom goals, you may elect to put more money into investments vs. vacation/toy/fun savings. If you have little or no debts, you have even more money to work with along these lines.

As mentioned earlier about how Passive Income Stacking™ = Time Stacking, when you have MORE money to systematically put toward savings/investments each month - so that it has the chance to grow and compound - you're potentially getting back several years of your wealth creation time. This is particularly significant if you'd like to retire sooner than later, or you're concerned about having the realistic financial ability to retire at all.

HOW TO FIND THE BEST
PASSIVE INCOME SOURCES

Realistically, you could search the business book section on Amazon and find an overwhelming amount of ways to make money. The challenge still remains that you're a busy person and only have a limited amount of time to not only consider extra income sources – but also the time necessary to evaluate and implement the business strategies you find. Not to mention, many are time-intensive which is often a deal killer if you have little extra time to begin with.

TRANSLATION: Many business opportunities are "Time Vampires".

That's why it's so important to first FILTER OUT the time/energy intensive income sources, and rather focus on "Passive Income Sources" that take less time to set up, manage, and that can ultimately be AUTO-MATED as much as possible.

That's a prime benefit of a passive income source vs. trading hours for money (a traditional job).

Good passive income sources can run on their own without your constant and personal involvement. This is how you can potentially have multiple passive income sources that you STACK – because they are self-running by design. Yes, some sources may take more managing than others, but it's different than being on the clock at a job.

YOUR OWN PERSONAL SOURCE OF PASSIVE INCOME GENERATORS TO CONSIDER STACKING

I wouldn't bring you this far on our Passive Income Stacking™ journey together to send you on your way to figure out what income sources make sense.

I know you're capable of such gold mining, but that too takes time and effort – and time is what most people lack…along with the additional income they desire.

The good news is, I can supply you with all kinds of Passive Income Sources to consider on a daily basis…and it won't cost you a single dime!

In fact, I've been supplying people with these kinds of income sources for decades. Let me share a little background on how I landed in the role of Passive Income Source supplier…

I'm a 3rd generation real estate investor. My Grandfather invested in his first "fixer-upper" property back in 1937 during the Great Depression in San Jose, California. He was also a chiropractor and all around opportunity-seeking entrepreneur.

One of his core values was helping people, and around the time of the Great Depression, people needed all kinds of help. He passed that core belief on to my father, along with the knowledge of how to run a real estate business. My father kindly shared all of that with me.

Before the Internet was mainstream, my father was written up in a national publication about some revolutionary marketing ideas he shared dealing with investing in discounted mortgages.

After that publication was released, we were overwhelmed with the amount of people asking us to share more ideas. That's when we started our free snail-mail newsletter and list of subscribers.

The demand continued to be so great to learn more of our techniques that we wrote and self-published the first book in the country on marketing for discounted mortgages titled, "How To Find All The Discounted Mortgages You Could Ever Hope To Buy".

After that books release we continued to be inundated with subscribers asking what else we were doing. We then wrote another real estate investing book, which had people requesting more ideas and the big snow ball has never stopped rolling.

What we soon realized was that we couldn't create enough Extra Income Source informational products on our own to meet the demand.

So we found other sources of really good strategies to earn Passive Income, and we shared them with our growing list of subscribers.

Fast forward to today and there are tens of thousands of subscribers that receive my FREE daily "Extra Income Sources" email newsletter.

Imagine having Passive Income Sources land in your inbox EACH DAY for you to consider. Talk about having the resources to potentially turn on and unleash YOUR

Fire Hose Money™!

If you're not already receiving my daily "Extra Income Sources" email newsletter - you can subscribe absolutely free at PassiveIncomeStacking.com/start-here.

To help provide more free information about the Passive Income Sources I find, I interview the experts of many of the income sources on my "Passive Income Stacking™ Show" podcast found at PassiveIncomeStacking.com.

Each episode focuses on one individual income source for you to consider, along with more information on the topic in that particular episode's "show notes" page.

The goal is to ultimately provide enough options so you gravitate to the ones that appeal to you. This way, after you've done your due diligence and want to move forward on certain potential income streams, you can begin STACKING them to hopefully generate the potential income and lifestyle you desire and deserve.

I've personally created different income sources for myself over the years including a mail order business, judgment investing, monetized blog, books/products, Google AdSense, Cost Per Click and Cost Per Lead Advertising, affiliate marketing, rental houses, REITs, and dividend producing investments to name some.

As mentioned earlier, I officially fired my day job back in 2004 and have been Passive Income Stacking™ ever since. As I write this I'm adding more to my Stack as I find income sources that inspire me. I don't think I will ever stop because the way I do it provides me with the income to enjoy the freedom it also creates.

Because of that…

PASSIVE INCOME STACKING™ = HOPE STACKING

These are challenging financial times we live in. Debt is rampant. Student loans are strangling many people's finances for decades. Medical bills are staggering. Bankruptcies are at record levels and even affecting older people to the point where they're "starting over" at later stages of their life.

Jobs are being downsized and lost forever. Employees are often asked to take on extra work duties while being paid less.

As all this is happening, good people are working harder, yet finding themselves with less money at the end of the month to pay all the bills that are due. In order to make ends meet, people take on more debt and get further and further underwater.

Sadly, the one income source that isn't paying people nearly enough to get out of debt and prosper (their job) – becomes that much more important because at least it's SOME money coming in. People then become servants to that one income source even if it means being treated less positively than they deserve, or worse.

The problem is these good people often feel like the pay from their job is as good as their financial life will ever be. So they stay in this same situation – almost as if being in quick sand – for years at a time or until they're eventually let go.

The result is… more people with depression; divorce due to money strains; stress; bad health; and ultimately a life that's not nearly as much FUN as I want yours to be for you!

So let's wipe ourselves clean of those last few paragraphs and consider a COMPLETELY DIFFERENT PATH FOR YOU!

Are you in? Yes?! Good, I was hoping you'd say that!

Are you beginning to see how Passive Income Stacking™ = Hope Stacking? With each ADDITIONAL passive income source you activate, you're adding another piece of hope to your Financial Empire. Yes I said FINANCIAL EMPIRE!

Listen, the ONLY reason why you might have been discouraged about your finances before reading this book is because you may have more money going out, or that's owed, than is coming in. As a result you might be going further in debt without much hope in site…UNTIL NOW!

From THIS very moment going forward - with each new Passive Income Source you choose that FLOWS IN to you each month - you have one more thing to be VERY HOPEFUL about, right?

With some of that extra money coming in, let's consider sharing a portion with others who need it too! I'll never forget how I felt back when I had very little money. I used to wonder if things would EVER get better. I'd sit in my mobile home and think to myself, "If things ever do change, I will never forget this awful feeling because others must be feeling this way too, and they're hoping and praying for some kind of help". Because I kept true to my word, it now feels so good to be able to finally GIVE… both with my time, and with donations.

PASSIVE INCOME STACKING™ = CHARITY STACKING

I'm sure there are causes near and dear to your heart. Maybe it's to end certain diseases, protect children, feed the hungry, keep animal's safe, etc.

One thing I've learned over the years, during times when I've felt broke, and others when I had a few bucks, whenever I donated my time or money to a good cause, it ALWAYS left me feeling better!

Have you ever experienced that feeling after giving something to someone? I'm sure you have! The old adage is true, it IS better to give than receive. I've always said that when I give I'm actually being selfish because I get so much JOY from it.

The good news is that when you have passive income sources that are stacked and kicking out money, you'll be able to funnel some of it to your most cherished causes where you think it will do the most good. Some may even be tax write-offs, so that's a win-win!

Now you have one more impactful reason to add to your "Why" when it comes to putting effort towards Passive Income Stacking™…giving to those in need. The more you receive, the more charitable donations you can STACK.

PASSIVE INCOME STACKING™ = FREEDOM STACKING

The extra income you stack each month not only adds to the HOPE that you now have…

You're also stacking the chance for REAL FREEDOM in your life.

With only one income source (your job), you're at the mercy of OTHERS. That takes most of the control away from you. That's RISKY because they control your financial life…and that impacts your personal freedom as well. No wonder we get stressed out!

Once you begin successfully activating and profiting with the passive income sources you choose, each one can potentially stack more CONTROL and FREEDOM into your life…until ultimately you're at the mercy of NOBODY when it comes to your finances. That results in you having the ULTIMATE FREEDOM to do what you want when you want!

Remember, you're not alone in this journey. Each day I will send you an email with Passive Income Sources to consider Stacking – absolutely free.

You can listen to my free Passive Income Stacking™ podcast episodes for more in depth details on extra income sources that just might get you VERY EXCITED.

THE ROAD AHEAD MAY BE BUMPY FOR OTHERS - BUT NOT FOR YOU!

We are entering uncertain times. The job market is evolving to phase out workers and pay those that remain even less when possible.

Companies are looking out for THEIR bottom line without a sincere concern for the bottom line of the employees who make the company run successfully.

Debt is at an all-time high, both personally and with our local, state and national levels of government.

The cost of living seems to climb each year.

NOW is the time to RECOGNIZE a financial MODEL that's here to SERVE YOU!

You now know the true power of Passive Income Stacking™…

Passive Income Stacking™ = Control Stacking

Passive Income Stacking™ = Time Stacking

Passive Income Stacking™ = Money For Debt Stacking

Passive Income Stacking™ = Power Stacking

Passive Income Stacking™ = Wealth Stacking

Passive Income Stacking™ = Hope Stacking

Passive Income Stacking™ = Charity Stacking

Passive Income Stacking™ = Freedom Stacking

YOUR PERSONAL
FINANCIAL STAIRCASE

Now that you have an initial understanding firmly in place, let's dig deeper into how to assess YOUR personal financial situation, and then help design a Passive Income Stacking™ path that can better serve you.

The way I've always viewed the Passive Income Stacking™ model is with a "Look In and Look Up" approach. That simply means I first look inward to see where I am currently with my finances, and what beliefs and actions got me to this point – good or bad, right or wrong. It's all about assessing and redirecting our financial course so we're pointed in the direction we'd much rather be heading.

Next I "Look Up" to the financial goals I have and the possibilities of reaching them based on certain actions I could CHOOSE to take. For me that is the ACTION of uncovering and implementing new income sources to add to my Stack.

Before we take one more step on this Passive Income Stacking™ journey together, you must first determine where you are currently in what I call a "financial staircase".

Imagine for a moment that you're standing at the base of a staircase. In FRONT of the staircase, before you ever get on the first step, is your DEBT. This would be credit card debt, student loans, car loans, medical bills, etc. We're not talking about a home loan…yet. For now we're just talking about revolving monthly debt that only seems to linger and grow.

Interest charged on our debt is one of the biggest things that keeps us down financially, often for LIFE. Its money compounding in REVERSE as it's designed to not only keep us in debt, but keep our debt GROWING due to the very HIGH amounts of interest being charged.

"RULE OF 72"

Let me first give you a simple to understand example of how money compounds and grows *for us*, and then we'll talk about how that can happen in REVERSE *to us* with interest charged on *bad debts*.

The rule of 72 shows, generally speaking, how long money you currently have invested will take to DOUBLE. To calculate this, simply divide the interest you're EARNING on your money into the number 72, and that's a ballpark of how many years it will take your money to double.

For example, if you're making a 7% annual return on your *money invested*, it will take approximately 10 years for your money to double. That's when your money is GENERATING more money for you…that's *good interest*. That's how your money helps you build wealth.

Okay, now let's focus back on interest charged on your debt…

When credit cards charge as much as 27%, that's how your *money owed* helps SOMEONE ELSE build wealth. I'd rather see your money build wealth for YOU!

Start thinking of impulse purchases in this way. Can you go out today this second and find an investment that will pay you 27% safely? If you answered "No", then why would you offer this kind of investment to a credit card company run by complete strangers? They flat out don't deserve that much of your money…or the future effort it will take you to pay it back and the stress you'll feel for years until you do.

Consumer debt erodes your ability for money accumulation. In order for you to be able to take the first step up Your Financial Staircase, you must first get out of *bad debt*.

That's where your FIRE HOSE MONEY™ comes in! Like I mentioned earlier, once you've got your passive income rolling in, you can begin pointing it in the direction of the debt that you'd like to pay off the fastest.

You can be systematic and strategic until each of your bad debts are paid off completely. Whew…that will be a GREAT feeling, won't it?

As soon as your bad debt is eliminated, you can begin to do what's necessary to take your first step up Your Financial Staircase. The first step represents EMERGENCY MONEY. That's money you don't touch unless there's an emergency in your life. It could be a car repair, medical expense, or the loss of a job where you need money to pay your overhead, food, and other bills.

You should consider creating this emergency fund at the same time you're paying off your bad debt. That way even when you're still in debt you've got an emergency fund waiting to help you should you ever need it.

Just to clarify, I know I first said you must get out of debt before you take steps up your financial staircase. But, when it comes to emergency money, it's important to always have a stash of cash you can access at any stage of your life – regardless of where you are financially, so you don't go further in debt as you're trying to eliminate it.

Once you're out of debt, it's important to begin pointing your FIRE HOSE MONEY™ in the direction of your financial staircase so you can actually begin to climb up until you're at the top.

Our financial staircase is unique for all of us. Your steps could include…

- Child's education
- Save more for retirement
- Generate more income so you never outlive your money.
- Have more Freedom and Fun!

YOU get to decide what each step of your financial staircase represents.

Either way, the second step - above emergency money - is savings that can GROW to best accomplish the goals you have for each step as you climb UP.

If you're reading this and you have no debt and have a ready supply of cash for emergencies, this is the step you'll be paying more attention to. That's because the more FIRE HOSE MONEY™ you can point to your savings and investments, the faster and larger it has the chance to grow.

This type of savings could fall under such saving and investing choices such as a ROTH IRA, ROTH 401K, Bank CD (especially when interest rates are high), Index Funds, REITs, etc. I'll explain what these are shortly.

Having a number of places like these to consider parking your money where it grows nicely, depending on the market, can be good targets for your FIRE HOSE MONEY™.

Of course that depends on your research, risk tolerance, and the economic cycle you're planning within. (I'm not giving any investing advice here. Consult with your attorney, accountant, and investment advisor before investing.)

You might be wondering how much money you'll need in savings before you reach the top of your financial staircase?

Before I address that, let me first ask you a question. Do you know what the BIGGEST financial concern of older retirees is? The fear they might *outlive* their money. If you stop to think about it, that would be a VERY scary place to find yourself.

Many older retired people live on a fixed income. That means they might be receiving a social security check and nothing else. Or maybe they have other money coming in such as dividend distributions, annuities, bank CDs, or other savings they can tap into.

At the same time, the cost of living is often going UP. So whatever money they have saved becomes that much more important and essential. That season in life focuses on "Capital Preservation". These people may have cash reserves that they can tap into from time to time, but when it's gone it's gone, and then they're left wondering how to pay the bills that seem to be going up each year while their fixed income stays around the same.

To add to the challenge of potentially out living their money, medical advancements enable people to live longer. So for these retirees, they live in a state of "lower economic mental health" for far too many years of their life.

With that fact in place, the top of YOUR financial staircase doesn't mean having "just enough" until you have nothing. It means HAVING MORE THAN ENOUGH…for the rest of your life!

The steps in the middle of your staircase, above the first step which is your emergency money, represent the AMOUNT you have growing in different areas until you've reached the top of your staircase.

Being at the top means you're COMPLETELY debt free, with a free and clear home, and plenty of money to last the rest of your life and beyond.

Plus, it means you've got enough in savings and income to no longer need a regular job. If you want to keep working fine, but it's because you WANT to and not because you HAVE to.

To get to the top level of your financial staircase, you will have calculated how much money your basic needs and fun lifestyle will cost you each year, so at a minimum you know how much money you'll need to provide that.

As you're enjoying retirement your Passive Income Stacking™ should still be in place so you have NEW MONEY coming in. This way your saved money has a chance to GROW even more over the years and DURING your retirement…no matter how young or old you decide to *responsibly* retire.

Most people's idea of retiring is finally quitting their regular job with enough money saved up to use for the rest of their life. Unfortunately many people end up retired and worried that they may run out of money if they live a longer life. Worrying that you're going to outlive your money is no way to live!

With Passive Income Stacking™ in place the goal is to still be generating and growing money WHILE YOU'RE RETIRED.

Yes, you may indeed have some happy relatives or charities when your estate finally gets divided up, but that means they will smile every time they think about you!

THE 2 MACRO CATEGORIES OF PASSIVE INCOME STACKING™

There's a direct correlation of where you are on your financial staircase – and the 2 macro categories of Passive Income Stacking™.

Once you understand the power of both, you'll begin to see how you can ultimately USE THEM IN TANDEM to help you achieve the freedom you desire and deserve.

PASSIVE MACRO CATEGORY 1. MONEY CREATION:

This is the stage when you are generating NEW MONEY. You're establishing passive income sources where money is first CREATED, as opposed to money you already have that you're trying to grow.

You might decide to generate this new money by activating a number of different strategies that I share that are passive in nature.

If you find yourself in front of your financial staircase standing in a pool of debt, chances are that Macro Category 1 may help you. If you aren't able to pay off your debt right now, then having extra PASSIVE cash generators would probably help, right? This is particularly true if you find yourself with *more month* at the end of your money.

If Macro Category 1 sounds good to you but you're not exactly sure how to create new money passively *yet*, don't worry because like I said that's what my Passive Income Stacking™ podcast and free Extra Income

Sources newsletter is all about. I'll be bringing you passive income sources to consider adding to your Stack on a daily basis from this point forward!

PASSIVE MACRO CATEGORY
2. MONEY COMPOUNDING:

This is the stage when you've got existing money, or you're taking money you've created in Macro Category 1, and you're making it work FOR YOU so it continues to grow on its own. This could be money you've put into Index Funds, Dividend Stocks, REITs, Bank CD's or other invested capital opportunities you choose. As a quick reference…

- An Index Fund buys all (or a representative sample) of the securities in a particular index. For example, when you buy shares of an S&P 500 index fund, you're buying a piece of all 500 companies in that index. An index fund value (cost per share) rise and fall – based on values of stock prices for the companies in that particular index. This helps spread out your risk vs. buying individual stocks. There's also less buying and selling of stocks in an index fund vs. a mutual fund. This helps keep your fees down so you can keep more of your profits.
- Dividend Stocks pay out a percentage of a company's profit to shareholders. You can benefit when the share price of the stock goes up above the price you paid for it, AND with dividend distributions.
- REIT is an acronym for "Real Estate Investment Trust". Once again you buy a share that represents a certain collection of real estate investments. You can benefit when the share price of the REIT goes up above the price you paid for it, AND with dividend distributions.
- Bank CD or Certificate of Deposit. You give the bank a certain amount of money for a certain time, and they pay you a predetermined amount of interest that you receive once the term has been met and your money is returned. During periods of low interest rates, little

interest is generated. However, during periods of inflation and higher interest rates, nice returns on your money may be realized. Many people put their money in banks because they aren't aware of other options, and because they appear safe. Either way, if you choose this route look for a bank that's FDIC insured so *some* of your money may be safe.

(These are just a few examples of *some* investments available to consider. Always consult with a qualified accountant and investment advisor before investing in any of these or other potential income sources.)

SYNERGY BETWEEN THE 2 PASSIVE MACRO CATEGORIES

Here's the big picture view:

You're taking the NEW MONEY you've generated in Macro Category 1…

And you're putting it into passive investments that you choose inside Macro Category 2 so your money COMPOUNDS AND GROWS to help multiply your Passive Income Stacking™ efforts.

By taking the new money you've PASSIVELY generated to pay off debt - and then to PASSIVELY invest with, you're essentially creating your own *systematic money machine*. If you'd like to take some of the money being kicked out from your investments in Macro Category 2, and invest it *back* into your new money efforts in Macro Category 1…

You've effectively created a *two-way-money-machine* SYNERGY between Macro Category 1 and Macro Category 2.

Synergy #1 - Passive Macro Category 1 "new money" goes into Passive Macro Category 2 investments.

Synergy #2 - Some of Passive Macro Category 2 *investment-profits* can go into Passive Macro Category 1 new-money generation *costs and overhead* if you choose. Or you can leave that money in investments so they COMPOUND and GROW, and instead use new-money profits from Macro Category 1 income sources for growing more new-money sources.

The good news is once you reach this point, you can choose where you think your money would best be utilized.

Stop for a moment to reflect how far you've come here. You've just uncovered a unique system that helps you find and establish PASSIVE income sources, and then how you might consider growing and COMPOUNDING your money even more.

Reflect for a moment how YOUR retirement years might look when you have money continuing to be GENERATED and COMPOUNDED! As long as you don't over extend yourself financially, and barring unforeseen circumstances, you can forget about outliving your money.

I cover more details on this in my Passive Income Stacking™ SYNERGY training. SYNERGY is how you establish a *balance* between Passive Income Sources in each of the Passive Macro Categories to best fit your Goals.

I hope you're starting to get an idea of how POWERFUL this can potentially be for you. These two categories become even more *strategic* when you factor in where you stand on **your financial staircase**.

Debt is always in front of the first step of the staircase. As your passive income sources stack up and help you pay off your debt faster, you begin to take your first step up your financial staircase.

Each step UP is another step toward your financial freedom.

The big picture view of your personal financial staircase shows you getting out of debt, generating savings, then investments, until you're completely debt free with plenty of money being generated and grown to retire and enjoy life – that would represent the top of your financial staircase.

Now imagine YOUR personal financial staircase. Where are you standing?

Are you in front of the first step surrounded by debt such as credit cards, car payments, school loans, medical bills, etc.?

Do you have your debt pretty well under control and you're a step or two up the staircase by having some emergency savings and also money in investments inside your ROTH IRA, ROTH 401K, or rental houses, etc.?

As a quick reference…

- A ROTH IRA and ROTH 401K are accounts designed to offer you tax savings. They're usually free to create at places like Schwab.com and TDAmeritrade.com. Once established, they're your own accounts used to buy and sell stocks, index funds, mutual funds, etc. They're designed to allow the gains on your trades to be tax *deferred*. Again, consult with a certified accountant before you create and invest with these types of entities so you fully understand their potential benefits within your financial plan.

Or are you around the top of your staircase because you're debt free and just looking for great passive income sources to help grow the money you already have so you never run out - as you continue enjoying the freedom in your life?

There's no right or wrong answer. To start making progress up your financial staircase you must first establish where you are right now.

If you need to find passive income sources to help pay off debt, go into your emergency fund, and grow your nest egg, you may want to find passive income sources that generate money FOR YOU while you're off doing other things - (Macro Category 1).

If you find you have plenty of money, your goal might be to find more passive income sources to Stack so your money grows and compounds faster and safer - (Macro Category 2).

THE 4 MICRO CATEGORIES OF PASSIVE INCOME STACKING™

There are 4 Micro Categories of Passive Income Stacking™…

Micro Category 1. Your Goals:

Why do you need the money you're hoping to get with Passive Income Stacking™? Is it to get out of debt, buy a new car, save for a child's education, save for retirement, etc.?

You may have more than one goal. There's no set number here, it's just what your situation requires. First simply establish your reason/s for needing this extra money.

Micro Category 2. Timeframe to Reach Your Goals:

How soon would you like to accomplish the goal/s you've established above?

If you've got a lot of debt your answer is probably "YESTERDAY", right? Sadly there's no magic wand you can use, that's not how life works. So you must be realistic in the timeframe you choose.

However, the more passive income sources you successfully Stack that are in the top of your 80/20 results, the shorter your timeframe may have to be. (More on the 80/20 Principle in a moment).

Micro Category 3. Time Available to Work on Passive Income Stacking™:

How much time do you have to devote to your financial stair case and Passive Income Stacking™ efforts?

Obviously the more time you have that you're using wisely, the better chance you have to accumulate extra income sources to Stack.

Once you've establish how much time you have available to dedicate to Passive Income Stacking™, you'll be able to better evaluate income sources you may want to consider pursuing. For example, those that will take a lot of time vs. those that are quicker to set up and manage.

If one income source will take a lot of time to establish on your part, and after further study doesn't seem to have the chance to be very profitable considering the time you'll have to dedicate, you can stop your efforts right there.

If another income source seems to be simple to establish with the same income potential as that above, you may want to investigate further.

Maybe another income source you're considering is quick to establish and appears to have a lot of profit potential. Bingo, you may have found a winner to consider adding to your stack!

Everything worthwhile takes effort and this is no different. But remember, you're worth it and I know YOU can do anything you set your mind to!

Micro Category 4. Potential Income for Each Source:

Not all passive income sources are created equally as indicated in the 80/20 Principle that we'll soon discuss. Some *could* make a lot of money and others may make very little if any.

Let me be perfectly clear about something from the start. You can do an Internet search right now for "Passive Income Sources" and find several potential sources to consider. You'll notice many pages list a lot of the same passive income strategies. Some are good, others are downright hokey.

When I suggest income sources to subscribers inside my free daily "Extra Income Sources" e-newsletter, I'm not suggesting taking online surveys for money or seeing if stores owe you money. Not that these aren't viable ways to earn a buck, but they're not nearly as EFFICIENT and PROFITABLE as other choices.

That's when a better understanding of the 80/20 Principle as it pertains to Passive Income Stacking™ comes in as your benchmark for the Goals, Timeframe, Time Available, and Potential Income for each source you're evaluating.

WHAT ARE YOU TRYING TO ACCOMPLISH?

In order to best pick income sources to Stack you must first establish what you want them to do for you within a certain time frame.

This is your "Passive Income Stacking™ Plan".

Within your plan you're probably trying to accomplish a number of different financial goals such as pay off debt, create an emergency fund, buy a new car, pay for a child's education, save for a great vacation, buy some toys, add to your nest egg, invest so you never outlive your money, etc.

When you're considering your plan, look at it through a lens of *EFFICIENCY*.

First, determine which Passive Macro Category you're in:

- **New Money Creation**
- **Existing Money Compounding**
- **Both**

Next, evaluate each passive income source you're considering within the 4 Micro Categories:

- **Your Goals**
- **Timeframe to Reach Your Goals**

- **Time Available to Work on Passive Income Stacking™**
- **Potential Income for Each Source**

Next, establish the *MISSION* for each passive income source you consider based on:

- **Efficiency to establish**
- **Ease of use, monitoring, and running**
- **Potential productivity – PROFITS**

Finally, I'd like to add one more thing to consider here:

- **Virtual Assistants**

If applicable, could some of the work to maintain the passive income sources in your stack be outsourced to virtual assistants? Only do this with money you can afford to spend on passive income sources that are profitable enough to warrant it. This could free up more of your time to evaluate more income sources, maintain the ones you have, or just enjoy more of your free time.

Okay, treat all these as your *FILTERS* when considering a passive income source to Stack. With these criteria in place, you now have the beginning of a Framework within which to begin considering passive income sources you gravitate towards.

After each potential income source goes through your filter, some will probably be discarded due to failing this simple filtering test. Rejoice when you pass on a potential income source you may have initially found attractive because that means it may not have been worth your time or effort. It also may not have been profitable enough within your own personal guidelines.

That means your filtering system is doing its job…Nice work!

When you consider each potential passive income source you gravitate towards, you can now feel better because you have this organized filtering system in place.

To protect the valuable time you have available for your Passive Income Stacking™ efforts, determine how hands-on each of the sources will require you to be.

Remember to review your goals and the 4 Micro Categories on a regular basis, and update them when necessary.

Diversify so not all of your passive income sources are in one "basket" in case that sector of productivity should ever dry up. Remember my Father's words, "Don't be a one trick pony." That always reminds me to be looking for new and *unique* passive income sources to consider putting through my filter.

YOU'RE ONE STEP CLOSER TO CLIMBING YOUR FINANCIAL STAIR CASE!

Without this Passive Income Stacking™ filtering criteria in place, you could spend far more time spinning your wheels instead of choosing better suited income sources to help fulfill your desired goals.

You now have a Passive Income Stacking™ plan to use to help you in your pursuit of building the most profitable and time efficient passive income stack as possible!

THE 80/20 PRINCIPLE FOR PASSIVE INCOME STACKING™

There is a principle in nature that dictates 80% of results come from a certain 20% of actions. I'm merely the messenger of this principle. Books have been written on it. Businesses will often say that 80% of their income comes from 20% of their customers. It happens in many areas of life.

Think of Macro Category 1, money generation, as your Passive Income Stacking™ *business*. Now think of your income from it within the 80/20 Principle. Once you have income sources coming in, you can determine your biggest money earners. There's a business expression, "Feed the stallions, starve the ponies". That merely means spend more time on your business WINNERS, and very little if any time on your business LOSERS.

With that knowledge you can save time by spending little time on passive income sources that appear to be money losers, and focus more of your attention on potential passive income WINNERS. Once you've established the activities that produce the best profits, you can be harvesting and ultimately collecting more of these types of passive income generators when possible, in different niches preferably to create diversification and lower your overall income risk.

It's like panning for gold because you will quickly review potential money generators until the gold nuggets begin to reveal themselves. Once you hone your money income seeking skills, you might be able to better uncover those that can generate the most cash with the least amount of effort, generally speaking. You'll then be looking for only the income generators that have the highest odds for monetary success.

In other words, you're looking for the 20% of passive income sources that will be generating 80% of your income within Marco Category 1. As you better determine which kind of money generators are your biggest winners, you can spend more of your time looking for these types of income sources.

THE 80/20 PRINCIPLE CAN BE LAYERED TO DETERMINE THE BEST OF YOUR TOP WINNERS!

Imagine for a moment that you have several passive income sources STACKED and generating money for you. Within your stack you should be able to determine your top 20% winners that are kicking out generally 80% of your passive income.

Now separate only your winners within your top 20% and determine which of those are your SUPER-STARS. Yes, just like in professional sports where all the players are better than most everybody on the planet at their chosen field, there are some that are ridiculously more talented than most all of the other players.

Going back in time it was Wayne Gretzky in hockey, Michael Jordan in basketball, Tom Brady in football, you get the idea. You don't have to like these athletes or the teams they played on, but chances are we'd all like them on OUR team if we were trying to win.

That's the same with passive income generators in Macro Category 1 that far exceed others in your stack. We'd all like a hockey team filled only with players as good as Wayne Gretzky. That's not possible when it comes to sports teams, but with passive income you're in control of which passive income sources make it onto your "team". You can add sources and cut sources and never get involved with sources unless they have the potential to be in your Top 20% if you like.

Once you've determined your top 20% of income generators, simply evaluate which are the best within that group. Next, determine the characteristics that allow them to create this type of EXTRA income compared to the other passive income sources in your stack. With this new information, add this to the criteria within your initial filtering system when first considering an income source. This is high-level criteria you'll now have to use that are unique to your chosen niche.

(I'm only referring to Marco Category 1 here, because activating the 80/20 Principle within Category 2, money compounding, can add more risk and that's not what this is about.)

THE 80/20 PRINCIPLE FOR "TIME REQUIRED"

When you have more than one passive income source generating money, you'll have a "control" to base the amount of time necessary to establish, monitor, and run your income sources. Many of your Macro Category 2 passive income sources should require far less time than Macro Category 1 passive income sources. Because of this, only compare the time requirements of income sources in the same Macro Category.

As you get more hours under your belt, you'll begin to gather knowledge about what activities are more productive than others. A lot of this has to do with the amount of time you have available to spend, and then how you best allocate your time so you're making the best use of it.

You can be cutting out distractions during the time you have to devote to Passive Income Stacking™ so that more of it is used for doing the most potentially profitable activities. This is one half of the equation. The other half is how much time a passive income source requires. If the income source is in your top 20%, that time may be warranted. If it's in your bottom 80%, you may want to consider if that income source is worth your time.

You want to work SMARTER and not harder. You do that by spending 20% of your time doing the things that create the most income. Once you've determined which activities these are, you can devote more of the 80% of time you have remaining to them. This way you're working smarter by doing the things that will hopefully produce the most income for you.

You've now improved your filter even more to better understand what makes an income source in your chosen niche a potential Super-Star, and how to best focus the majority of your time getting the most out of your current winners while you're looking for more potential winners to add to your Stack.

If Passive Income Stacking™ was a sport, these are some of the things the super-stars would most likely be focusing on to be the best they can be. You now have even MORE skills to begin honing during your quest for Financial Excellence.

"HOW TO MAKE YOUR FIRST MILLION DOLLARS" CLASS

Over the years as I've learned more about money, and money creation, I've often thought how great it would have been when I was in high school had there been a class called, "How to Make Your First Million Dollars".

Out of the classes students could elect to take, I have a feeling most would want to take this class, right? I sure would have because back then I didn't have a clue about money. Sadly, many people go the rest of their life in the same boat without ever learning much more about money other than how to finance things and figure out how to make minimum payments that often last for years.

Imagine that first day of class back in high school as you walk in trying to look as cool as possible. You spot a seat in the back row and sit down so you can go unnoticed. You're remaining calm but inside you're actually excited because you're thinking this class is all it will take to put you on the track to easy-street. Everybody around you is thinking they're on the brink of becoming bona fide millionaires.

The teacher walks in wearing shorts, a t-shirt, and sandals. He has a smile, a tan, and seems to be in a great mood. He starts off by telling stories about some of his fun hobbies like being an extra in Hollywood movies, playing in rock bands and hanging out with rock stars, traveling around the world, regularly volunteering at a zoo and taking care of animals like rhinos, giraffes, and hippos.

Within these stories are celebrity meetings and plenty of jokes and fun experiences. You instantly find yourself loosening up and starting to enjoy the moment. You're not sure if this guy knows anything about money, but it sure seems like he knows how to live a great life.

The teacher then asks this question, "By a raise of hands, who here wants to learn how to become a millionaire"? You see everyone raise their hand.

He then asks, "How many of you are willing to work REALLY hard every day and sacrifice all your good times to become a millionaire?" Hardly any hands go up this time.

He then asks, "By a raise of hands, how many of you would like to become a millionaire by scraping up a couple hundred bucks each month and have it grow while you're off doing other things that you enjoy?" The mood in the room got fun again as all the hands went back up.

He asked, "Okay, do you think you can figure out a way to generate $200 each month for the next 38 years?" You nod in agreement.

He then dropped this bit of knowledge..."Did you know that if you invest $200 each month into something that generates a 10% return on your money, that after about 38 years you'd have $1,000,000? You would be about 52 years old by then." That seemed like an eternity away, but it didn't sound bad.

He continued, "Would you rather have your million dollars in 28 years?" Of course being a 42 year old millionaire sounded even better. "Then find a way for your $200 monthly investment to generate 15% each year and you've got it!"

He then asked, "How many of you want your money sooner than that? Would you rather have your million dollars when you're about 39? To do that invest $300 a month into something that generates a 15% annual return and you're a millionaire by that age."

He closed with, "Now if all this sounds too good to be true, but you'd still like your money sooner, let me spring this one on you. If you were to invest $400 each month into an investment that generates a 15% annual return, you'd make your first million dollars in just over 23 years. You'd be about 37 years young. Now, if you only made 10% on your $400 monthly investment, you'd still reach millionaire status in about 31 years. You'd be about 45."

"You know class, sadly there are plenty of people who work their entire lives and have hardly any savings. To make things worse, they buy things on credit, and instead of having their money earn interest *for them*, they PAY interest to *others* each month.

So let me ask you class, which one of these examples do you want to be, a millionaire in the making or a person strapped for cash forever? The next time you go shopping online or in a store, stop for a moment and really consider if that purchase and the interest connected to it is worth taking money away from your 'Monthly Millionaire Fund.'"

He then simplified things even more. "Alright friends, who here wants to learn how to do this in 2 simple sentences? All of you, okay that's good.

Sentence one… find a way to generate $200-$400 extra dollars each month, the simpler the better.

Sentence two… find ways to make your money grow PASSIVELY while you're off doing other things.

Are you all still with me? Good! Okay let's continue…"

Alright, let's break away from the story here while I ask YOU a question. If you had a class like this back in high school, do you think it might have made an impact on the rest of your financial life? Me too! By the way, the teacher in this example is me. Living in Arizona, that's how I dress much of the time, and those are just some of the things I enjoy doing.

If you're now somewhat intrigued and find yourself wondering how to accomplish what's covered in Sentence One and Two, you already know it!

Sentence one is Macro Category 1: Money Creation.

Sentence two is Macro Category 2: Money Compounding.

The good news is, you know more than the fictitious class because if you've read all the pages that preceded this one, you've got the beginnings of a plan already in place!

HOW TO BE RICH WITH A SMALL INCOME

Let me share a story with you…

First, as I write this I have more money than I've had at pretty much any time in my life. There are people that have a lot more money and possessions than I do, but I'm doing alright. The funny thing is though, when I think about a time when I actually FELT rich, its back when I lived in my old single-wide mobile home back in the 1990's. How is that possible you might be thinking? Believe me, I wonder the same thing.

I mentioned earlier how I bought my mobile home for the full price of $5,500. Let me share the rest of the numbers so you can get a better feel for the dramatic financial effect it actually had.

When I first moved to Phoenix, Arizona back in 1992 from California, a friend I'd known since high school and his girlfriend wanted to move there too. We all shared an apartment. My friend was the stage manager for the heavy metal band Anthrax and his girlfriend worked for them too. They would be on tour a lot and rarely at our apartment, although they paid for 2/3 of the rent. Our rent was $610 and my share was about $203.

That worked well because I wasn't making a lot of money at the time. After living together for almost 2 years, one day they came to me and said they wanted to get another place for just the two of them because they were going to get married. That made sense to me. After a couple weeks I found myself with two weeks left to find a place to live.

I had read a book on how to invest in mobile homes and it showed the exact kinds to buy for the best investment. With that knowledge I set out to find one at a good price.

After driving around several mobile home parks in the Phoenix area, I came across the mobile home that I showed you earlier for sale.

It was owned by a lady who owned it free and clear, meaning there was no loan outstanding. She was asking $5,500 cash which I felt was a pretty good price at the time. She had a very new refrigerator, and a washer and dryer that were included. I paid her and the home was mine.

I didn't own the land that the mobile home was sitting on however. I still had to pay lot rent which included water and garbage pick-up. The lot rent was $203 and change. As you may recall, that's about the same exact amount I was paying in rent for my share of the apartment. That was a happy coincidence!

At that time in the economy there were a number of vacant lots in the mobile home park so I went to the manager and said I was considering moving the home, and was wondering if they would give me some free months lot rent if I stayed. They gave me 2 months for free which added up to about $406. That essentially knocked the price of the mobile home down to around $5,100. That plus the nice appliances helped keep more money in my pocket.

In addition to the $203 lot rent, I also had to pay for utilities which didn't add up to much, maybe about $50-$75 a month. So for under $300 a month total, I had a free and clear home. That was cheaper overhead than if I had a large house that was free and clear because with that there's the expensive taxes, insurance, and utilities that would add up to a lot more than $300 a month. So I quickly realized this new scenario was special.

I lived in that mobile home near the railroad tracks for 6 years! I never made a lot of money during that time but you know what? I *FELT* more financially free during that stage of my life than I ever have. I guess it's because my overhead was so low, and even though I didn't have a lot of money, I had <u>more than enough</u>. I didn't have any debt, so after taxes and a little bit of monthly overhead, the rest went into savings.

I've never been a big spender, so I usually had enough money for the things I wanted. Because of that, my PERSPECTIVE of money at that time was that of *real freedom*...EVEN THOUGH I MADE LESS MONEY THAN MOST EVERYBODY I KNEW!

The big take-away so far in the story is, *don't over extend your finances* to the point where you're always in mental-stressful-hustle mode. That stress is a killer, literally. By being out of debt and having more money at the end of the month than I needed, even though I made very little, I just FELT rich.

There are plenty of people around us that APPEAR to be wealthy. Easy credit has allowed us all to drape ourselves in nice clothes, an expensive car, a desirable home....AND PLENTY OF DEBT.

There's an expression for that, "All ranch, no cattle." That simply refers to people's material lives being a façade; a fake reality. In contrast, the financial reality I had in my old mobile home wasn't much, but it was REAL! I had no debt. My home was my own. The overhead was low. Even though I wasn't making much, I had MORE than enough.

Yes being rich means one can buy things. But it's also a way of life because responsible money management affords FREEDOM. Many people that make far more money than most spend UP to that amount, so in reality they have less money than those who make better money choices who earn less. Just do an Internet search for athletes who have spent all their money.

I realize that in today's social media world it's easy to get wrapped up in feeling inadequate compared to others that are posting their *fake reality*. I'm suggesting you see through that and don't play that game. Instead, get out of debt, collect emergency savings, then investing capital. At the same time, don't outspend what you're making so you can save and grow your money faster. That's the reality I want for you, and YOU DESERVE IT!

Listen, I saw all the great cars driving by me as I drove to my mobile home. I saw people with truly amazing lives, and you know what, that's okay! There will ALWAYS be someone with MORE…always! We can't win that game, but we can win within our own game.

Now, let's go back to when I was living in my single wide mobile home trying to figure out my next move. As you know I lived there for 6 years. My overhead was LOW LOW LOW. That gave me some wiggle room to try to make certain things happen. I already had a mail order business that was morphing into an online business. That helped a lot and still does.

I had a rental house during that time and I'm sure my tenants had no idea they were living a higher lifestyle than I was. I'd drive over to the house, perform my landlord duties, then drive back to a less desirable part of town where I lived. I always got a good internal chuckle about that at the time. I knew the tenants were providing the money necessary to make the home loan payments, so it was fine with me!

During that time I established and began to perfect what would ultimately become my trademarked Passive Income Stacking™.

So why did I share all this with you? It's because I wanted to show you, firsthand, that it doesn't matter where you are on your Financial Staircase right now. You're simply at the beginning of this journey. Of course you may be well along your way too. But if not, peck away at those bills, don't outspend your income, let other people play the "fake-rich" game until you truly begin to *feel rich* even if you aren't making a lot of money. Believe me the feeling is worth it and so are YOU!

I'm not suggesting that you have to get a single wide trailer like I did. That was my situation; my opportunity. Find the opportunity that's around you right now and see if working it makes sense. At the very least you now have Passive Income Stacking™ ready to work for you and that's a lot.

HOW TO MAKE THE NUMBER "10" WORK FOR YOU

Here's a simple example of how to generate a savings that keeps growing to levels that may put a smile on your face, and HOPE back in your heart.

We're all familiar and comfortable with the number 10. That's because the "decimal numeral system" uses 10 as its base. This is the most common system used for numbers so it's no wonder we're familiar with the number 10.

We use a 1-10 scale when grading all kinds of things. We're used to a collection of ten being called a decade, and a collection of ten decades being called a century.

You can add a "0" after the number 10 and it goes up ten times to 100. Pretty simple when you think about it, right?

So how do you get this very simple number to work *for you*? In this scenario, we're going to use the number 10 in reference to TIME. 10 months to be exact. It's less than a year, so it FEELS like less time. Because so much of our money woes are in direct response to our EMOTIONS and the result of over spending because of them, the *feeling* that 10 months isn't as long as a year is significant.

First figure out how much money you can save each month for the next **10 months**.

$10 saved each month for 10 months = $100

$50 saved each month for 10 months = $500

$100 saved each month for 10 months = $1,000

$200 saved each month for 10 months = $2,000

$300 saved each month for 10 months = $3,000

$400 saved each month for 10 months = $4,000

$500 saved each month for 10 months = $5,000

$1,000 saved each month for 10 months = $10,000

As you can see, over the next 10 Month Savings Cycle you can get your savings rolling. Considering we'd all like to feel more SECURE by having more money saved, this is a simple method to activate.

Once you figure out how much money you have to save each month, you'll most likely find you can live without it. Sometimes you barely feel it's missing, especially if the way you're coming up with it is by stopping frivolous spending on things you don't really need, which we all do by the way. These would be purchases that sooth your EMOTIONS so you feel better in the moment, if only temporarily.

The irony with this savings program is, you'll FEEL BETTER now and in the long run, with less guilt than buying relatively meaningless things that you no longer remember after 10 months have passed.

This "10 Month Savings Cycle" is a way you may choose to save more money starting right now, TODAY. It's simple, it's effective, and dare I say *relatively painless*, unless you're really sacrificing a lot for your savings program. This should just be one more way for you to get ahead financially. You can use money you've already got to start with, and then add to it with your Passive Income Stacking™ efforts going forward. What you ultimately do with these savings is for you to decide.

With this idea firmly in place, what would happen if we added another "10" to our TIME FRAME? Let's find out!

If you were to save the same amount as above for 20 MONTHS you'd have…

$10 saved each month for 20 months = $200
$50 saved each month for 20 months = $1,000
$100 saved each month for 20 months = $2,000
$200 saved each month for 20 months = $4,000
$300 saved each month for 20 months = $6,000
$400 saved each month for 20 months = $8,000
$500 saved each month for 20 months = $10,000
$1,000 saved each month for 20 months = $20,000

I've tried to give a wide range of numbers here depending on where you find yourself financially. If you can save more each month, that multiplies these numbers even more. The fun part of this is, if you've got a couple nickels to rub together, you can be doing this every month over the next 10 Month Savings Cycle starting RIGHT NOW!

"DIRTY DOLLARS SAVINGS PROGRAM"

When I was young back in the 1980's I used to work at a men's clothing store in the mall where I lived in California. It wasn't quite like the mall immortalized in the movie, "Fast Times at Ridgemont High", but it was sure close.

Among the cast of characters I worked with was an older gentleman named Clarence. He was most likely in his 70's, but to me he seemed much older and wiser. He told me once about a way that he saved money. He said, "Whenever I have a dollar bill that's dirty, I put it in a jar." He called it his "Dirty Dollars Savings Program".

Evidently I had shared that story with a single buddy of mine back in the day, because years later his *wife* told me about how *he* does this thing called "Dirty Dollars" where he saves dirty dollars that come his way.

I couldn't believe my ears as she recited the whole process, just like my friend Clarence had originally told me while working together years before. Clarence is no longer with us, but his kind and helpful words can now live on with you too. (Please share them with others in Clarence's memory…the smartest guy I knew in the mall!)

Okay, your mission, if you choose to accept it is…right now locate a jar, box, can, or baggy to put the *Dirty Dollars* you find going forward. I'm guessing you can find at least 10 each month to add to your monthly savings program. If you feel a little daring, consider doing this with dirty

$1 and $5 bills. Could you even throw in a dirty $10 or $20 bill once in a while?

Sure, be generous, after all, you're not spending it frivolously, you're strategically SAVING and paying yourself, and for that you can FEEL GOOD!

What's this, *positive emotions* connected to your money situation? Yes, and you can feel this Good Mojo each time you "tuck-a-buck-away"!

DIRTY DOLLARS + 10 MONTH SAVING CYCLES = MONEY ACCUMULATION

This is just bare bones, simple savings build-up we're talking about. When combined with "Passive Macro Category 2 - Money Compounding", you have a potential way to get that money to COMPOUND and GROW.

Remember the Rule of 72 we talked about earlier? That's when you take the percentage of interest being generated on your money and divide it into the number 72, and generally speaking, that's how many years it takes your money to double. That means you have the chance for the saved money on the right side of the "10 & 20 Month Savings Cycle" examples shown a few pages ago to potentially grow even larger.

You can also combine your "Fire Hose Money™" with your "10 Month Savings" and "Dirty Dollars" to have even more money to work with in ways that you feel will benefit you the most.

When it comes to positive money emotions, you can now feel even better once you effectively activate your...

- **Passive Income Stacking™**
- **Fire Hose Money™**
- **10 Month Savings Cycles**
- **Dirty Dollars Savings Program**

Look out *FINANCIAL FREEDOM*, here YOU come!

EARLY PAY-OFF PLAY BOOK

One of the many positive bi-products of Passive Income Stacking™ is what I refer to as, "Take Back The Term". You've probably heard the phrase "Price and Terms". Price is pretty straight forward; it's what something will cost.

When you use *financing* to help access money for the cost of something, that's when the *terms* of that financing comes in…and the negative effects of INTEREST that we're all too familiar with.

Let's first create a firm foundation of what negative "terms" we're dealing with on *consumer financing*, and then how you might consider creating an Early Pay-Off Play Book for each of the debts you want to eliminate.

One place we see "terms" mentioned a lot is how car dealers promote the "price" of a car. The dealer often promotes how much a car will cost by only mentioning the monthly payment amount. "For only $299 a month this car can be yours." That payment, and plenty of interest, will be paid for several years.

Generally speaking, the *Terms* of your car loan is the amount you borrowed, the interest being charged, the late fees you will incur if your monthly payment doesn't get to the lender on time, and the amount of time you'll make your monthly payments until your loan is paid off.

When you buy a *house* using credit, the time-frame of the term of your loan will be longer than a car loan, because a house purchase requires a larger loan amount. This way you have more time to pay monthly payments that you can afford.

Generally speaking, the *Terms* of your house loan is the amount you borrowed, the interest being charged, the late fees you will incur if your monthly payment doesn't get to the lender on time, and the amount of time you'll make your monthly payments until your loan is paid off.

If you have *credit card* debt it works a little differently. Your credit card company charges interest, but the amount of time you have to pay back what's owed is open-ended, meaning there's no set amount of time that you have to pay the money back. That's because credit card companies are more than happy to continue charging you exorbitantly high interest for as long as you're willing to pay it, and why wouldn't they? To keep from over extending themselves, they cap the amount you can borrow.

Generally speaking, the *Terms* of your credit card is the credit/cash limit, the interest being charged, and the late fees you will incur if your monthly payment doesn't get to the credit card company on time.

Now that we've covered some common consumer debt terms, let's focus on the TWIST that lenders often create that *shift more of the terms in their favor*, so we end up giving them even more of our hard earned money for the privilege of borrowing theirs.

Scenario: Let's say you have a rich uncle who has a lot of money. One day you find yourself in a money-pinch, so you ask your uncle if you can borrow $5,000 that you'll pay back monthly over the next 5 years. Your uncle agrees, but requests you pay 10% interest.

He says he'll work up the numbers so each of your payments will include a portion of Principal (the amount you are paying back), plus a portion of the Interest you're paying. (When scheduled loan payments include principal and interest it's referred to as "Amortization".)

However, in addition to the Terms of your $5,000 loan for 5 years with 10% interest, your "kind uncle" structured the amortization schedule to have Font-Loaded interest.

That means a LARGER portion of each of the earlier monthly payments you'll make during the 5 year term will go towards INTEREST! As time progresses, more and more of your payments will then eventually go toward the *principal* amount owed.

That means you're NOT paying an even amount of interest in all your payments. You'll be paying MORE interest in your earlier payments, resulting in the BALANCE of the principal amount you borrowed taking longer to be reduced, within your 5 year term.

You figure, okay, why not, I need the money and it's going to take me the entire 5 years to pay back the loan anyway, so you go ahead with it.

But what happens if you come into some money after paying your uncle for 2 years and you want to pay back what you owe? You'll be surprised to find out that the amount you originally borrowed from your uncle hasn't gone down much because most of your early payments went towards INTEREST. Sadly, you'll still owe him a lot more than you thought you would.

If you knew how your uncle's Front-Loaded Interest would negatively affect you if you were to ever PRE-PAY your loan, you may not have agreed to that *TERM* in the first place. **However that's EXACTLY what most car and home loan lenders do with their financing!**

If you wouldn't get into a loan like this with your favorite rich uncle, why would you do it with financing companies? The answer for all of us most of the time is to access the money needed to get what we want because we don't have the money currently to use.

Alright, the reason I've gone into so much detail here about Terms is so we're both on the same page. With this simple understanding you'll hopefully be able to better assess your own consumer loan scenarios. Now it's time to consider how to best construct and activate an "Early Pay-Off Play Book".

Because car and home loans usually use front-loaded interest as part of their terms, it means we're paying a LOT of interest in the beginning years of the term. If you have a house with a loan, go to your account on your lender's website and look at the "History" for the loan payments you've made and see how much of your monthly payment actually goes towards your PRINCIPAL (the amount you borrowed and owe). The lender is taking so much interest in the first 20 years, it's no wonder it takes 30 years to pay off! Plus it adds so much extra money to the original cost of your house.

Before you activate a plan to pay off a car or home loan earlier than your loan term, first see if there is a "Pre-Payment Penalty". As if front-loaded interest isn't enough, lenders sometimes push the loan terms even more in their favor by charging you a *fee* to pay off the loan before they want to stop charging you interest.

Even though lenders offer a valuable service by offering money to those who need it, it can be VERY expensive over the long term. Make sure to check if there is a pre-payment penalty with the loan you're interested in paying off early. If there is, check the numbers to see if it would even make monetary sense to pre-pay the loan.

If there's not a pre-payment penalty on your loan, you may want to consider creating your own "personal term" to pay it off early. I call this, "Taking back the term."

This is something you'll figure out on your own based on where you want to point your Fire Hose Money™. Like we covered before, you can start paying more than your regular monthly loan payment amount so the extra goes to PRINCIPAL ONLY each month on the loans you want to pay off the fastest.

HERE'S HOW I DO IT...

When I'm making a monthly car payment or payment on a particular house I'd like to pay off sooner, I send 2 checks. One is for the regular monthly payment amount that I usually make. The second check is for the

EXTRA amount that I want to go toward *principal only* (the amount that's owed). I write "PRINCIPAL ONLY" on that check. On the payment stub I write the amount of the 2 checks. Next to the principal only amount I again write "PRINCIPAL ONLY". I'll then highlight the words "principal only" on the check and payment stub with a yellow highlighter.

I do this because unless otherwise informed, sometimes lenders will credit your extra payment as if it were a normal type of payment that goes towards principal AND interest. I bring it to their attention and then check each month to make sure it was credited properly.

CREATING MY NEW "PERSONAL TIME FRAME" TERM...

With a calculator I figure out how much principal is still owed and how much EXTRA I can afford to pay toward the loan each month. I divide only my extra payment amount into how much is still owed to give me a ball park of how much quicker I may be able to pay off the loan. Yes, I'll still be paying interest, but the amortized *interest* amount will be going down faster each month as more of my payments go toward *principal*. Plus my regular payment amount includes *some* principal as well, so it's a good one-two punch!

Lenders would LOVE for us to make every payment and use the entire amount of time to pay back a loan so they're paid the MAXIMUM AMOUNT OF INTEREST. By creating your own "personal time frame" term you'll essentially be TAKING BACK CONTROL of some of the loan terms that are weighted so heavily in the lenders favor.

Consider the "terms" of each consumer loan you currently have outstanding. Next, create the best "personal time frame" term for each one.

These are your *custom plays* to be entered into your "Early Pay-Off Play Book" so you can eliminate that debt as quickly as possible.

Remember, life happens. If one month you can't make the entire extra payment, that's okay as long as you're able to start back up again the following month, or as soon as possible.

This is a process. There is ALWAYS light at the end of the tunnel! Whatever financial challenges you may be facing right now, they too shall pass because better times are right around the corner for you.

With your Early Pay-Off Play Book firmly in place and activated each month, you're essentially expediting how quickly you get to the end of your debt tunnel where you'll finally be out and enjoying the sunny weather!

HOW TO RETIRE WITH PLENTY OF INCOME WHILE YOU ENJOY YOUR LIFE

The thought of "retirement" for most people means they've generated and saved enough money to have the chance to retire from their regular day job. With the money they've earned over the years, they've hopefully made good investment decisions so they can live off the money they've saved.

For many, this reality falls short because they never saved and invested enough money that will ultimately be used to COMPOUND and kick out the needed funds to retire in style. Sadly, these people never have enough money to retire in the first place. They literally have to keep working forever, or until they can be taken care of by others, if that's even a possibility.

The traditional way of earning income means you're required to trade your hours for a pay check. That income goes away as soon as you retire and stop going to work.

That's not the case with the Passive Income Sources you've worked to create, maintain, and stack. Assuming the money from those sources continues to come in on a regular or semi-regular basis, and it more than covers your overhead and will for the foreseeable future, you can continue making money while you're retired REGARDLESS OF YOUR AGE OR SITUATION.

That's important because like I mentioned earlier, the biggest fear for those that are retired, especially if they're older, is that they will outlive their money. Some people retire from their regular day job, but are forced back to work to pay for health insurance. In that type of scenario, will those people ever really be able to retire?

The way to take the mystery out of retiring while you **continue to generate income** in the 2 Passive Macro Categories of Passive Income Stacking™ (money generation and money compounding), is to first create a monthly budget for your retirement lifestyle goals.

Once you know how much money you will need to be generating during your retirement, you'll know the MINIMUM your Passive Income Stack will need to produce on a **regular basis** from that point on. Of course, with the knowledge you're gaining, you can always *Add To Your Stack*.

Your goal should always be to try to create more passive income than your budget requires to cover unexpected needs and circumstances. Also be sure to create passive income sources in different ways and niches so you have diversification when some income sources decline or stop altogether.

Here are *some* of the items to consider when creating your budget:

Groceries

Clothes

Household Goods

Mortgage (Principle, Interest, Taxes, Insurance)

Utilities

Water

Garbage

Internet

Phone

TV Services

Car Loan (hopefully this will be paid off)

Car Insurance

Gasoline

Car Maintenance, Tax, License, Registration

Health Insurance

Doctor Visits (Primary, Dentist, Optometrist, etc.)

Medicines/Prescriptions/Vitamins

Long Term Care Insurance

Term Life Insurance

Umbrella Insurance

Vacation Fund

Tithes

Pet costs

Donations

Entertainment (Movies, Restaurants, Fun)

Treats For Animals

Chocolate :-)

PART 2

PASSIVE INCOME STACKING™ SOURCES

55 PASSIVE INCOME SOURCES TO GET YOUR JUICES FLOWING

Before you go through the pages that follow, please view the income sources as a practice-pad for evaluating future income sources you consider going forward. I designed these as merely examples of what's out there. I share far more in my daily "Extra Income Sources" newsletter and "Passive Income Stacking™ Show" Podcast.

In order to best pick your income sources to Stack, you must first establish what you want them to do for you within a certain time frame. This is your "Passive Income Stacking™ Plan".

When you consider your goals, look at them through a lens of EFFICIENCY.

First, determine which Passive Macro Category you're focusing on...

- Passive Macro Category 1: Money Creation
- Passive Macro Category 2: Money Compounding
- Or Both

Next, evaluate each passive income source you're considering Stacking within the 4 Micro Categories…

1. Your Goals
2. Timeframe to Reach Your Goals

3. Time Available to Work on Passive Income Stacking™
4. Potential Income for Each Source

Next, establish the MISSION for each passive income source you consider based on…

1. Efficiency to Establish

2. Ease of Use, Monitoring, and Running

3. Potential Productivity - PROFITS

Use these as FILTERS when considering a passive income source to Stack.

It's important to understand that not all passive income sources are winners. Some will take too much time to establish and activate, some will take too much time to monitor and run, and some won't make enough money, if any at all.

With that in mind, you BEGIN to understand that FILTERING is extremely important when considering passive income sources to evaluate and activate. You don't want to waste your precious time on potential income sources that aren't going to help you achieve your most desired goals. (For reference see "The 80/20 Principle for Passive Income Stacking™" section of this book.)

That's why it's so important to look at my daily "Extra Income Sources" e-newsletter and listen to "The Passive Income Stacking™ Show" podcast, because I'm always looking for new and exciting passive income sources to share with you.

On the following pages are 55 passive income sources presented in alphabetical order. These are here merely to give you an idea of SOME that are out there to consider, if for no other reason than to start PRACTICING your own *personal filtering criteria.*

Some of these may appeal to you, while others will undoubtedly be put into your "PASS" category. That's perfectly normal. You don't need or want to activate every POTENTIAL income source you see because you will ultimately be spinning your wheels so much that you think this doesn't work. That couldn't be further from the truth.

That's why I bolded the sentence earlier saying, "It's important to understand that not all passive income sources are winners. Some will take too much time to establish and activate, some will take too much time to monitor and run, and some won't make enough money, if any at all."

What you're looking for are WINNERS – income sources that are more SIMPLE to evaluate – activate – run – and that are more PROFITABLE than others that may tempt you.

Whether or not any of the following income sources resonate with you, view this as an exercise for opening your mind to the possibilities that are all around you. This in itself will begin to attract more potential opportunities into your awareness.

As you look through the income sources that follow, ask yourself these questions…

- Is this something that interests me?
- Is this something I could be passionate about so the activity is kind of fun?
- Does this look like it will take too much time to Evaluate?
- Does this look like it will take too much time to Activate?
- Does this look like it will take too much time to Oversee and Run?
- Does this look like it might not take TOO much time to establish?
- Does this look like it might not take TOO much time to oversee and run?
- Does this look like it might have POTENTIAL to be PROFITABLE?
- After all these questions are answered, does it look like a potential WINNER?
- If applicable, could some of the work be outsourced to virtual assistants?

Run this filter, and the ones discussed earlier as you look at each of the income sources included here. You can always add more filtering criteria, but this is a good start to practice with.

There are far more passive income sources out there in the world than are listed here. I share several more with my subscribers each day. But the INITIAL filtering system is the same.

Now is the time to put on your EVALUATOR HAT as you scan through each source. Consider this PRACTICE for all the additional passive income sources that I'll continue sharing with you online.

Please realize that many of these may represent a passive income source NICHE where you might find other passive income sources *within it* to piggy back and Stack. It's within the niche that you'll begin looking for passive income sources that might meet your 80/20 Principle filtering.

This is just the BEGINNING. Don't be discouraged if none of these pass your test. That's absolutely okay! You're honing your skills to what a good or GREAT passive income source niche MIGHT look like to YOU.

Don't worry, I'll be here every step of the way!

What follows is a quick overview sampling of 55 potential passive income sources that currently exist. They're listed in no particular order other than alphabetically for you to easily find and reference. You should be able to do an online search for any of these to gather more information should you choose to do so...

1. ADSENSE

AdSense is also known as Google AdSense. Google offers advertising to paid advertisers to promote their business and products.

To help Google extend their advertiser's reach, they offer ad placement to online publishers like you. That simply means if you have a blog, website, or YouTube videos, etc., you can have relevant ads for your niche appear.

You get paid when people click on those ads, or it can be based on how many views the ads have gotten, depending on how you have it set up.

The types of ads vary and should continue to evolve over time. Some of the ad formats are Text, Image, and Video.

The ads are created by the advertiser, so you don't have to worry about that. You're simply allowing Google's ads to appear within your content.

Google reviews the ads to make sure they're high quality and fit within your niche and content.

To help give you control, if there are ads you don't like you can block them. You can also choose what type of ads you like and where they'll appear.

Set up is relatively simple. As this is written it's free to create an account at https://www.google.com/adsense/start

2. AFFILIATE MARKETING

If you can create an online way to get in front of people, you can potentially be making extra passive income offering other people's products or services for a percentage of the sale you referred.

Affiliate programs are offered by those who want to get more traffic and business for their product or service and are usually free to sign up for.

After you sign up you'll be given a unique affiliate link that points to a webpage. When you share that link and it's clicked/tapped, that referral is tracked back to you. If the person who clicked the link should make a purchase, you would get a commission. Commission amounts vary.

First, do an Internet search for "Affiliate Programs". Find ones in niches you're interested in. Within the ones you feel would be good to pursue, determine the highest paying commissions and the offers they represent. Look for offers you feel good about that would be of value for the people you're referring. You want to offer good things so people feel your recommendations are helpful.

Places you can offer your affiliate suggestions include a blog, website, podcast, email, etc. Be sure and follow FTC rules of disclosure when suggesting affiliate links.

Some niches pay more than others. Categories such as finances or investing can offer affiliate commissions as much as 50%. That can really add up when your link points to higher priced offers.

Many times your link will point to a page where your referral is offered something for free in exchange for their email address. Once the source has your referrals email address, your referral will be on *their* mailing list and usually offered different things to buy in which you would receive a commission for if a sale was made. Besides the income, another benefit is someone else handles the sale and customer service.

3. AIRBNB™ PROPERTIES YOU DON'T OWN

You may have stayed in some kind of luxury rental property before.

The experience is like stepping into another lifestyle in an exotic part of the world without having to own the property.

Many people are willing to pay for this experience and there's proof considering how popular these kind of rental properties have become.

Now put yourself in the property owner's shoes for a moment. They possess what could be expensive to own and maintain property. To recoup some of their expenses, they've opted to rent it for the potential income, but they're still at the mercy of their MARKETING.

That's where you come in to help take that "burden" off of them.

There are trainings I offer on my website that show you how to locate luxury rental owners who will often be more than willing to let you list their properties on Airbnb™ type websites. The result is, YOU get to keep a portion of the income generated.

The more properties you have under contract, the more potential income.

To help with the "passive" aspect of this, you simply need to know how to outsource and automate the business to avoid working full time hours, yet earn a consistent monthly income for as long as you have the relationship set up with the property owner.

Learn how to set this up for yourself at…

PassiveIncomeStacking.com/income-sources

4. AMAZON

Amazon offers you several ways to potentially set up passive income streams.

Every business in the world would love to have active and passionate customers that are looking to open up their wallet and spend money like those that are browsing Amazon 24/7.

The good news is, you can get listed on Amazon for free and start tapping into the steady stream of viewers, IF they can find you.

Because of this ready source of viewers and buyers, there are a few ways you can choose to attack this.

1. Sell your own items on Amazon. Do you have a book or product that you've created? Amazon offers a source of customers who might be interested.

2. Amazon has an Affiliate Program. You can sign up for free and begin offering links to your subscribers and followers. Like we discussed earlier, when people you refer through your affiliate link buys something, you earn a commission.

You can get set up and running in as little as one day. Plus you'll have over a million products to consider sharing with your followers.

This is another way you can be quickly set up to monetize your website passively.

As this is written, Amazon's website says you'll be getting up to 10% in advertising fees, and that you'll be able to earn advertising fees from Qualifying Purchases, not just the products you advertised. Check their affiliate information to make sure you have their most recent policy.

5. APP CREATION

You can create apps that people download for free. If you're not a techie you can outsource the creation for a fee. Far more free apps are downloaded than premium apps. Both have their merits, but if more people are willing to access a free app, let's consider some ways to generate income that way.

1. Advertising. Affiliate promotions can be offered inside your app. Make sure the affiliate offers are "App Friendly" so you know you're advertising affiliate promotions that will be tracked properly back to you so you get your earned commissions. Some of the type of ads within apps are...

"Cost Per Click" (CPC) - you earn money when someone clicks an ad.

"Cost Per View" (CPV) - you earn money when people watch video ads.

"Cost Per Install" (CPI) - you earn money when an advertised application gets installed by your viewers.

2. Purchases. Users can make purchases inside your app. A few types of purchases are...

"Subscriptions." These can be renewing or non-renewing subscriptions. People can also unlock some functions or content within the app for a specific length of time.

"Consumable." Consumables are one-time use products like virtual money or points used in mobile gaming.

"Non-consumable." These can help the *efficiency* of the viewers free app *experience* such as permanent ad blocking. This would be how to make money without ads if your app is free.

6. BATTING CAGES

If you live in an area with a lot of youth and adult sports including baseball, this may be something to consider.

Yes, to make it passive you will need to train managers to run the facility, but compared to other businesses like restaurants with daily food preparation and health guidelines to follow, there is not as much day to day preparation required. You will need to load up on insurance in case of injuries. Some of the services you can charge for are…

- 1 hour cage rental
- ½ hour cage rental
- 1 hour lesson
- Camps for teams or groups
- Pitching Clinics
- Hitting Clinics
- Birthday parties
- Merchandise, etc.

You can offer membership levels that offer member discounts on the services above such as…

Non Member: Full Price

All-Star Member: $45 per month. Receive certain level discounts.

Elite Member: $85 per month. Receive discounts higher than All-Star Members.

This is something to consider in areas where people are spending money on sports and leagues. For areas of the country with a lot of rain and snow, this may be the type of business that generates a fun past time out of the elements, and a place for children and adults alike to enjoy good and healthy activities.

7. BLOG

A blog is a way you can create a presence online in any niche or niches you like. That's significant considering a blog can be monetized and accessed 24/7 from anywhere in the world.

What are you passionate about? What gives you joy when you talk about it? Your blog can be your personal passion project! Plus you can have more than one in different niches in an effort to maximize profits.

WordPress.com is a very popular and versatile blog platform that offers free blogs, along with niche blogs for very reasonable prices. There are plenty of existing themes you can choose as the look and feel of your blog. Start thinking of the colors you'd like to represent your BRAND.

Go to Fiverr.com and have designers create your logo and other graphics for as little as $5 plus fees.

Your blog can be the "home base" where your online money making activities reside. You can post articles, videos, graphics, etc. Always offer something for free on your blog in exchange for the visitors email address so you can grow your subscriber list.

Once someone gives you their email address, you can have an email-autoresponder set up to automatically send emails to your subscribers on certain days and times. These emails can include both content your subscribers will value, and premium offers or advertising so you can earn money.

A blog is a perfect place for Product Pages, Affiliate Offers, and Advertising. Be sure to mention your blog online when posting on social sites and groups in the same niche as yours, this way people who are interested in what you offer can find your page and potentially become your loyal subscriber.

8. BOND OR CD LADDERING

Let's first start with simple definitions so we're on the same page…

A "Bond" is essentially a loan you're making to a company or government. Your money is helping to fund something. There is an "end date" for your loan when the bond matures and you are to receive your principal back, plus a premium which would be your profit.

Some bonds have incredible risk while others such as those from large established companies and the United States government are presumed to have less risk.

A "Certificate of Deposit" (CD) is issued by a bank or credit union and considered by most to generally be safe. You are placing your money in this type of account for a pre-determined amount of time. Once the end date has been reached, you are to receive your principal back plus interest.

These are general descriptions meant to give you the basic idea that both are choices where you may wish to park your money for the interest or yield being offered. That in of itself is a way to create some very passive income, particularly when interest rates are high. When interest rates are low, obviously less profit will be generated.

"Laddering" is when you own several bonds and/or CDs with different maturity dates. You can "time" your purchases to produce the dates throughout a year that you would like to use the profits as cash income.

By laddering, you're taking control of your "term" so that your income from these investments can be projected and planned.

Bond and CD laddering involve owning several different bonds and/or Certificates of Deposit. Each one matures at different times during the year. You can then take the profits from those investments as cash income during the year if you choose.

9. BUILD AN ONLINE GENERAL CONTRACTOR SERVICE & OUTSOURCE THE WORK

One time I bought a house that had zero landscaping in the front and backyard. I went online and found someone who advertised a landscaping service. He came to my house, got my suggestions, and then gave me a price that I agreed on.

What do you think happened next? Did HE come to my house and do the work himself? NO. He knew of different landscapers that specialized in different skills that he sub-contracted the work out to for a lower cost to *him*.

He did this with 3 different crews until the job was finished. The crews were happy because it offered them work they didn't have to pay marketing to find, and he was more than happy because he was paid a premium *by me* over what *he paid* the 3 crews WHO ACTUALLY DID THE WORK. He was the General Contract on this landscaping job.

Question: Would you like to be an "Online General Contractor"?

Imagine you have a free WordPress.com blog set up to offer a service or services of your choice. If someone wants to pay you for this service, you have a PayPal account ready to process the order. You then turn around and have a Virtual Assistant do the work for less, and you take what's left over.

You can even hire a different virtual assistant to oversee some of the customer service tasks to make sure things run as smoothly as possible.

Upwork.com is a place to find online freelancers. Go there to see some of the jobs they can fulfill and see if you can reverse engineer this model.

You can do an Internet search for "Virtual Assistants" to find companies that provide this service. Find ones that provide reliable services at affordable hourly prices.

10. BUY AN EXISTING ONLINE BUSINESS

The legitimate allure of an online business is that it works for you 24/7 and has a potential worldwide reach. The challenge for some can be getting an online business started and established to the point that it's generating consistent passive income.

If you've got the funds, one option may be to buy an existing business that's already up and running profitably.

To find listings for companies that offer online businesses for sale simply do an online search for "online business for sale". I did this and a few of the companies that came up were…

Bizbuysell.com

Clickstartdigital.com

Exchangemarketplace.com/categories

Exchange is Shopify's marketplace to buy and sell businesses.

If you don't find what you're looking for on these sites, simply keep searching for what's currently available for sale.

To keep things passive, you can find freelancers or virtual assistants to help with necessary day to day tasks.

You may want to explore the websites available in your hobby/passion niche to see how others are at least attempting to profit. If you find several, you may consider taking the best aspects of each to create your own unique version. In the early days, Sam Walton of Walmart used to visit his competitor's stores to find things they were doing that he liked to implement into his stores. You can do the same thing for an online business website you're building from scratch, or to help you better evaluate existing online businesses for sale that you may like to make an offer on.

11. BUY AND SELL DOMAIN NAMES

Domain names are merely website addresses. I remember when I was first getting online with my business back in the 1990's. It was like panning for gold as so many people were buying up domain names to secure for their own use. I bought my share as well through Godaddy.com.

Savvy entrepreneurs back then realized they could strategically purchase domain names that could have demand in certain niches with the thought of selling them for a profit. Here are the 7 most expensive domain names publicly reported…

CarInsurance.com — $49.7 million

Insurance.com — $35.6 million

VacationRentals.com — $35 million

PrivateJet.com — $30.18 million

Internet.com — $18 million

360.com — $17 million

Insure.com — $16 million

Now I'm not saying you're going to generate these kinds of numbers, but it is proof that people and businesses are willing to pay a nice sum for domain names they really want. The most I've ever sold a domain name for was $1,000. Someone reached out to me asking if I wanted to sell a particular domain name I owned that I wasn't using. I set my price at $1,000 and didn't budge. They agreed and I sold them the domain name.

Average domain names are pretty cheap. More specialized domain names demand a premium. The nice thing is there are websites set up for you to list domain names you own for sale.

Godaddy.com and Resellerclub.com are two websites where you can sell domain names. You can search their websites for more inside knowledge on how to do this, plus search online for more selling options. Remember to "protect your downside" by not paying much for the domain names you're trying to sell in case there's no demand.

12. BUY AND SELL ROYALTIES

Musical Intellectual Property is in demand these days from people needing all kinds of things from background music, theme music, branding, music for videos, movies, and more.

Online sources have popped up to meet this demand…for a price. When you "own the masters" of intellectual property (IP), you have something to offer and sell. Every time someone uses your music you get paid. You potentially have the chance to earn income over and over depending on the type of outlet the end user has in mind.

Owners of this type of intellectual property often get paid every time someone uses their work. They create an asset once, and then collect a payment over and over again. Imagine harvesting a niche of themed sounds, music, and sound bites that range from between 8 seconds to a couple minutes in length.

If you're looking to offer the music catalog you've collected and own the rights to, you can list individual downloads for sale on "royalty free music" sites. When you do an online search for that phrase you'll also find a number of sites to consider listing your music on for "one time purchases" to the user. Explore those sites to see what the criteria for purchase is so you can see what appeals most to you.

If you have the musical ability and desire, you can create this content for yourself to use and offer. If you're not as musically inclined, or you don't want to spend that kind of time in creation mode, you can consider paying musicians to create this kind of music for you that you will own outright. You can then offer this music to others to use for a fee or royalty.

Royaltyexchange.com is a website that has auctions that allow you to sell a portion of your IP royalties. Sellers receive payment from the successful bidder and investors receive a portion of the royalty revenue. Instead of offering the music, you may choose to *buy royalties* instead as a potential passive income.

13. CERTIFICATES OF DEPOSIT

We talked briefly about Certificates of Deposit (CD) earlier in "8. Bond or CD Laddering". That's when you have different CDs maturing at predetermined dates throughout the year, enabling you to receive income in a strategically planned way.

I'd like to go into more detail on CDs because so many people park their money in them. CDs are offered by banks and credit unions and are considered to be very safe.

The interest rate you're paid is usually higher than savings accounts and money market accounts, but you must leave your money in the account for a predetermined amount of time. If you take it out early you will likely pay a penalty.

You give the bank a certain amount of money for a certain time frame, and they pay you a set amount of interest that you receive once the term has been met and your money is returned.

Many people put their money in banks because they aren't aware of other options, and because they appear safe. Either way, if you choose this route look for a bank that's FDIC insured so *some* of your money may be safe.

During periods of low interest rates, little interest is generated. However, during periods of inflation and higher interest rates, nice returns on your money may be realized.

If you're looking for safety and a good return on your investment, remember the **Rule of 72**. Divide the amount of interest you're generating into the number 72 and that is generally the amount of years it will take your money to double.

If CDs are paying 2%, that means it will take your money approximately 36 years to double. If CDs are paying 7%, that means it will take your money approximately 10 years to double. If CDs are paying 12%, that means it will take your money approximately 6 years to double. When you combine high interest rate periods in the economy with the safety of FDIC insured bank CDs, it can be quite attractive.

14. CPA, CPC, AND CPL MARKETING

When you have a website in a particular niche, or an email newsletter with subscribers interested in certain topics, you're positioned similarly to a Media Company.

You're taking the appropriate steps to gather and supply information to your tribe of subscribers. They are engaged with what you're supplying in the niche they're interested in or possibly even *passionate* about.

With that connection and outlet established, you are in a unique position to leverage their attention, interest, and relationship by including some advertising in your messages by outside sponsors.

One type of marketing you may want to consider is CPA, CPC and CPL marketing.

Cost Per Action or Cost Per Acquisition (CPA) - You get paid when a person you referred performs a certain action like fill out a form.

Cost Per Click (CPC) - You get paid when someone you refer clicks on a link.

Cost Per Lead (CPL) - You get paid when someone you refer opts in to something offered by the advertiser.

The goal of the sponsor providing the ads for you to display is to generate leads and future sales to help grow their business. By aligning with these types of sponsors you have another way to monetize your efforts in a passive way.

Do an online search for "CPA Companies" or "CPA Networks" to find companies that place these types of ads. Once you have relationships with these companies, you can often pick the ads you feel would benefit your subscribers the most, while at the same time create advertising revenue for you.

15. DIGITAL PRODUCTS - DVDS, HOW-TO VIDEOS, SOFTWARE

The way I first got started in offering self-educational material was because of a book my father wrote decades ago called, "How To Find All The Discounted Mortgages You Could Ever Hope To Buy". He had been written up in a national investing newsletter about some revolutionary marketing techniques he shared with the editor to get more exposure for our business. People loved the content and reached out to us asking for more of our strategies. That started a snowball that continues to this day.

Being entrepreneurs, we created more informational products using different types of media such as books, videos, CDs, MP3s, etc.

The beauty of creating proprietary digital products is that YOU own the masters so you get to determine where the promotions and profits come from.

You may also decide to create an affiliate program that offers a percentage of the sale in commissions to those that refer your products to others. That's free marketing you can capitalize on for potentially years to come.

Once your products are created, you can have webpages that offer them 24/7. As you accumulate more products, you can offer upsells to increase the revenue you're generating from each order.

To create videos you can use your phone, or find an affordable camera and microphone online. To create audios simply write out some "bullet-points" that you'd like to cover and start talking about them in order. You can do a search for editing software to clean up any excessive "you know" and "ums" or other mistakes you may have made. That means there's no pressure because you can "fix it in the mix". You can find transcription companies to convert your spoken words into print for a digital book.

You can always find a good "intro" and "outro" voice over person at Fiverr.com to help make your video and audio projects sound even more professional. There you'll also find graphic designers for your cover art and logo creation.

16. DIVIDEND STOCKS

Dividends are payments made by companies to its shareholders. These payments can be made in cash, or in additional shares of stock.

It's a way for those who own stock in a dividend paying company to realize some of the profits in the company, up and above an increase in the price per share of stock.

When you buy dividend paying stocks and receive these types of payments, you are being rewarded with a portion of the profits. That can potentially help you in a few ways...

1. You can reinvest the cash dividends to grow the amount of shares you have.

2. You can take the dividend proceeds and invest in different stocks or other investments of your choosing.

3. You can take the cash to help subsidize your living expenses. This is particularly attractive to retirees trying to conserve their capital while generating income from it.

Other ways to invest in dividend stocks are through ETFs and Mutual Funds.

ETF is short for "Exchange Traded Fund". An ETF is a collection of underlying assets. There are several different types of ETFs available, and only some offer dividend stocks as a choice. The same is true of Mutual Funds.

Some differences between Mutual Funds and ETFs are...

Mutual funds are purchased at the end of the trading day, while ETFs are traded like stocks. Unlike stocks, these types of funds can have additional management fees, so be sure to assess those fees and expense ratios when deciding where to best put your money so your net gains aren't eaten up by overly exorbitant costs.

17. DROP SHIPPING

I first learned about Drop Shipping because it was a way for newsletter writers, before the Internet was popular, to promote our books. Because the Internet wasn't around yet, it was a great free way for us to get the word out to people interested in our "money creation" niche.

We would encourage newsletter writers to mention our products and take orders from their subscribers. They could keep 50% of the purchase price and the rest they would send to us plus the necessary shipping so we could send the product to their customer. In this example, we were the "drop shipper".

There was no cost for us to advertise. There was no cost or effort for the newsletter writer to create the product being offered. The customer received what they ordered in a timely manner. It was truly a win-win-win.

You can be offering drop-ship products that you didn't create, that you don't own, and that you don't have to keep in your inventory. Simply do an online search for "drop shipping companies" and see what is currently available for you to market and sell. First determine if there's demand for the products being offered. If not keep looking for drop ship companies until you find products that have demand. Without demand you're swimming upstream.

Next, calculate what the wholesale price and any other costs will be for the products you consider offering. Determine what you can sell the item for, at a discount if necessary to make sure you can make a profit that appeals to you.

Consider websites like Shopify.com to help you in your efforts. Be open to different niches to help spread out your reach to potentially create more passive income streams to add to your stack. If there's profit to be had, also consider a hobby niche you're passionate about so this new business venture can be fun.

Each time your promos for the products you choose to offer produce a sale, simply let the drop shippers fulfill the orders while you concentrate on generating more happy customers. You may also consider buying items in bulk if that makes monetary sense.

18. EBAY

If you can find items to sell, eBay.com gives you a chance to get them in front of people who are looking for things to buy 24/7.

Because of the nature of this book, the best way to produce a PASSIVE income with eBay is by HOW you're supplying the products you're offering.

If you have to go out every weekend looking for items to sell online, that's not very passive, unless you like to treasure hunt.

But, if you want to be able to create a consistent stream of sales, outsourcing product fulfillment may be your answer. If you're creating unique eBay shops that carry niche specific merchandise, continually being able to supply the items is key.

As mentioned earlier, Drop Shipping can help fill that role. If you decide to go the drop shipping route, eBay may be another outlet to consider marketing on.

As always, it's important to be able to offer items that have demand. If they can be found and purchased easily from other sellers, make sure to find items that you can acquire at a low enough cost to be able to undercut your competition's pricing.

For this to be a passive activity, your products must be acquired at deep enough wholesale prices, have a consistent supply, and if possible be sent by a fulfillment company so your time isn't taken up with packing boxes and driving to shipping establishments.

To get an idea of current demand for certain items, do an online search for "most popular auctions on eBay".

Here are a couple websites to help you determine what people are interested in -

Wuanto.com

Watchcount.com

19. ECOMMERCE STORE

If you currently have a brick and mortar store that sells items, consider adding an online presence for your selling EXPERIENCE. Let's face it, people can buy many things from several different sellers, both online and offline. What people often respond to is the FEELING they get when they engage with certain businesses.

Consider what Starbucks offers. Could you get many of the same type of products elsewhere? Of course! But those other places don't give customers the same FEELING they get when they walk inside Starbucks and experience the comfortable layout, the sounds of fun relaxing music, and those wonderfully familiar smells that make their emotions dance with joy.

People LOVE to buy. They HATE being sold. What helps them gravitate to certain businesses is the feelings they get when they engage with that business, either by walking in or opening up the attractive website with the items they want.

By incorporating your brick and mortar business with an ecommerce store, you EXTEND YOUR REACH. Your happy customers can visit you whenever they like. But that's not enough, you must GIVE THEM A REASON to do business with you.

That's where your ecommerce store can do things your physical location can't. For example you can offer something digital for free on your website in return for your customers email and any other information you'd like to gather. Maybe offer free coupons sent to them by email.

Once you have their email address you can give them reasons to buy from you with special offers, discounts, limited time offers, etc. Send out fun emails reminding them that you're here, and reasons to click a link to get to your website to view your latest and greatest offers. Your customers

LOVE to buy…give them yet another reason to love to buy from YOU with the relationship type experience that an ecommerce store (and the marketing it allows) can provide.

Of course, you can do this if you don't have a physical location as well, but I wanted to help expand your reach in case you'd like to maximize your marketing efforts even more.

20. ETSY

Part of the fun of Passive Income Stacking™ is that YOU are in control of what goes into your stack. Some choices may be cashing in on things you're passionate about, or are *good* at. If you've got a creative side and enjoy the hobby of making things, you can be selling your creations online (but let's take this even further).

If it's handcrafted, vintage, custom, or unique, it's on Etsy.com. Like we've talked before, if you can find unique things via wholesalers and drop shippers, this may be yet another outlet to consider reaching potential customers through.

However, I'd like to approach this a little differently. Growing up in school I took most all of the DIY type classes such as wood shop, metal shop, ceramics, and art. It was so much fun making things, but there's nobody but my mother who would have paid for any of it because I didn't have the best artistic skills.

If you are blessed with the ability to create wonderful things, maybe you would enjoy the process of making them for others for a premium. If you are an artist, maybe you can create unique pieces that you can mass produce to meet any demand you may be able to establish and grow.

Think BRANDING. Encourage interested people to sign up for your newsletter to receive behind the scenes "lessons and experiences" with new art projects you're currently working on. This way you can keep in touch, build rapport and solidify relationships with your followers and fans. Create videos explaining your thoughts and techniques as you create.

Consider offering "Patreon" specials to get people to pay you a monthly subscriber fee to get more up close and personal experiences with you. (More on Patreon.com later in this list).

You can make your art a MOVEMENT when you utilize websites like Etsy.com and then expand your brand, reach, and experience to move the people that believe in you the most.

21. FIVERR

In the beginning, Fiverr.com was a place that offered all kinds of services and products for $5. That is still the case, however with their massive success and appeal they've grown with the levels of services and pricing that sellers can achieve.

When I told a friend years ago about Fiverr.com his reply was, "I wouldn't do anything for only $5". The good news for people who feel this way is that you can now charge far more. The reason I'm mentioning this is because it's yet another platform to help get you in front of a massive audience if you have a product or service to sell, especially if that product relates to your service.

Let's say you have expertise in a certain area, and you have a service you provide based on that expertise. You can post what's called a "gig" on Fiverr.com for that service. You can brainstorm and try to come up with related services that you can also offer for an additional price. These could be stand-alone services, or better yet, upsells or package deals that would allow you to charge far more money.

In addition to the services offered in a specific niche, you may also consider creating digital how-to instructional products to offer. You would create them once, and have them to sell for possibly years to come. Delivery is a snap considering they're digital products.

Why would people buy these additional trainings? Because they're in a niche these people are actively looking for solutions in, and the more helpful content that provides these solutions the better. Plus, they will be time savers for your customers because all the information you've spent time gathering and presenting can be offered in one place by you.

Niche down your service and training's to create more offers. Consider raising your prices as business demands increase. Another "upsell" to consider is delivery time. You can offer to supply your services in say 5 days, or if people want it sooner they can pay extra for express delivery. Look to see what other upsells people are offering and make yours better and *collectively irresistible*.

22. FLIP HOUSES

You might think flipping houses is anything but passive, and in many cases you'd be correct. But there are a lot of ways to streamline your efforts with automation, outsourcing, and utilizing other investors to help reduce a lot of the heavy lifting.

Let's talk about a few different strategies that can better fit the Passive Income Stacking™ model when it comes to flipping houses.

There is software available that can "scrape" websites such as Craigslist.com for motivated home seller leads. That's significant because you need a home owner who is MOTIVATED TO SELL in order to have a chance of getting their house at a bargain price.

There is also software that can provide you with high equity leads, underpriced houses, pre-foreclosures, absentee owners, and out of state owners. These are the types of leads that also may be sources to pick up bargain houses.

When you have leads like these automatically delivered to you quickly by software, that's passive lead generation.

There's also software that will help you find private lenders and cash buyers. These can be essential tools to help you both acquire bargain houses, and sell them quickly to receive your profit.

At your fingertips is software that will provide information on houses such as photos, loan data, and more. It will help you dial in potential rehab costs and profits, along with email sellers using pre-written templates, and "fill the blank" forms to create a digital offer in minutes.

With software you can save a lot of time and gather a ton of information. Once you buy a house at a great bargain price, you can choose to sell it to a wholesale investor for a quick pay-day; sell it at a discount to a retail buyer for a bigger potential pay-day, or sell the initial purchase contract to another investor for quick cash. You'll find many more helpful real estate investing resources on my website CreatingWealthClub.com.

23. GET OUT OF DEBT

I remember hearing a story about an older man who was broke his whole life. Even though he worked hard and tried like crazy to get ahead, he continued being broke. Sadly, during all those years, his family felt his struggle and stress. They saw how hard he worked at a traditional job, trying diligently to get ahead.

His family was along for the ride as they too had to endure this financial scarcity, because it was theirs as well. Years went by and their lack of money was always a constant realization. After several years past, the man shared with a friend, "After a life filled with effort and hard work, I've finally come to the conclusion that the reason why I've always been broke is because of the INTEREST I've had to pay on my debts."

If you have any kind of consumer debt like credit cards, you know firsthand how much *interest* affects your ability to pay back your debt in a timely manner. The higher the interest rate charged on your existing debt, the harder it is to pay off. In many cases that high interest rate causes your debt to grow, especially if you're making minimum monthly payments.

Home loans are tough too because the interest is "front loaded", meaning you're paying more of it up front. People get so excited when they're able to get a home loan for a low interest rate, and for good reason. The reality is the lender has shifted that interest in their favor by manipulating the payments in the first 2/3 of the term to go towards an overloaded amount of interest.

If you have consumer debt, use your Fire Hose Money™ to help pay it off as quickly as you can. If you have a home loan, take a look at how much of your payment actually goes to *principle* (the amount you borrowed), and how much goes to *interest*. It may get you upset enough to encourage you to pay your house loan off sooner too.

Once you stop paying that lousy interest on bad debt that helps someone else get rich, you can use that money to help grow *your wealth* by investing it passively.

24. GROUP COACHING PROGRAM

Have you ever seen infomercials on TV that advertise some kind of book on money generation? Are those books expensive or affordable? They're affordable right? The reason for that is quite tactical, purpose driven, and focused. It's to uncover people who are essentially raising their hand saying they're interested in this topic, and are willing to open up their wallet to prove they are a buyer. That's a very valuable lead for those trying to sell things.

What do you think the REAL goal is for those types of offers? Yes it would be nice for the book sales to bring in enough profit to help pay for the infomercial production, television air time, and book publishing costs. It would also be nice if there was some profit left over. But what you're really seeing is the beginning of a strategic *funnel with upsells*. (We'll cover more on this subject in the "Product Funnels" section a little later.)

Here's a spoiler alert…the TOP of the funnel is often times some kind of very expensive one-on-one coaching program. It's more hands-on and time consuming for the coach, however quite profitable. Sometimes these can reach a six-figure price tag charged to the person being coached.

Who in the world would pay for such an expensive coaching program you're wondering? Someone with the willingness and ability to pay it; who wants the information and higher end attention and first class treatment while they get it. Presumably their goal is to take this new found knowledge and leverage it into more than they spent to get it.

A more passive way to charge a nice amount of money while working far less is a Group Coaching Program. If you have expert knowledge in a subject that's in demand, or can learn it, you may be able to offer group coaching for a premium.

You can charge what you like and see what the market will support. See what others are charging. You can do group phone calls, webinars where you teach and take questions, or have people fly in from around the world to partake in a group mastermind 4 times a year for as much as $25,000 per person annually. These types of programs are out there now.

25. HIGH YIELD SAVINGS ACCOUNTS AND MONEY MARKET FUNDS

If this seems a bit pedestrian, please remember that it really depends where you are on your Financial Staircase and how old you are. That's because when you get older you don't want to outlive your money. Many older people in that position concentrate more on *capital preservation* and living on the money being generated by the cash they've accumulated.

One other obvious aspect of this passive income source is the *percentage* of interest being generated. That depends on the market cycle.

During times of LOW INTEREST, many people think putting their money in these types of accounts is potentially safer, especially if the institutions are FDIC insured, while at the same time not generating much money overall from doing so or keeping up with inflation should it exist. They would be correct.

However, when interest rates are HIGH, it's a way to look pretty smart by having these safer types of investments generate much higher *yields* than we're often accustomed to when rates are lower.

Back in the late 1970's and early 1980's, interest rates were MUCH higher due to inflation. The returns these types of investments generated were worthy of bragging. I was too young at the time to realize all the benefits that could be had, but I will be ready next time we see much higher interest rates.

I remember someone who invested in Bank CD's back in those days telling me how great that was. Remember the Rule Of 72? Simply divide the number 72 by the percentage of interest you're receiving, and that's the amount of years it will take your money to double, generally speaking.

When interest rates are much higher, you can decide if a portion of your savings belongs in this type of passive income account.

26. INDEX FUNDS

My focus on low cost index funds sharpened when I read a quote made by famed investor Warren Buffet in Berkshire Hathaway's 2013 annual letter to shareholders. (Full disclosure, since that time I have become a shareholder as well).

Evidently he's instructed the trustee of his estate to invest in index funds after he passes away. Mr. Buffet shared this wisdom…"My advice to the trustee couldn't be more simple - put 10% of the cash in short-term government bonds and 90% in a very low-cost S&P 500 index fund."

I'm certainly not advocating you do as the quote above states, but it's worthy of notice considering the source. That statement led me to start uncovering more information about index funds, fund fees, returns, risk, and what they are in general.

One example of an index fund is a portfolio of different companies stock designed to track a certain market index. Index funds can also include bonds or other financial market types. A general goal for index fund companies should be to give investors a broad exposure to the market that's being covered, along with low fees and low portfolio turnover.

The S&P 500 Index tracks 500 large U.S. companies. Because the biggest companies are tracked, it's considered a benchmark of how the stock market is doing as a whole.

Because of the lower turnover with index funds, there are lower commission and management fees compared to many mutual funds. Considering large fees reduce overall return on your invested dollars, the lower fees associated with some index funds helps to make them even more attractive. As this is being written, Vanguard is a company known for having lower fees and they have plenty of investing choices one might want to consider.

When market cycles are strong and going up, index funds may look attractive, while down markets may create the opposite reaction. That's when dollar cost averaging becomes something to evaluate. Always consult with your advisor before investing.

27. INTERVIEW EXPERTS

This has the potential to be fun, impactful to your listeners, and a way to interview people you admire. If you have a hobby or passion project that has mass appeal, chances are other people are interested in it too.

You can create a free website using WordPress.com software. To monetize it you can include links to your own products in this niche, Google AdSense ads, affiliate products, along with other kinds of paid advertising. That's a pretty solid business model that can also be combined with email marketing.

Once you have your website up, start creating a list of 50-100 people you'd like to interview. Put together a few emails in advance so you have a systematic way to reach out to these people on a regular basis until you've made contact and have started the conversation.

You can reach out to the people on your list via Facebook, LinkedIn, email, or a phone call. Be friendly and let them know what you admire about their efforts and accomplishments. Let them know how much you'd be honored if they would allow you to interview them. Together you'll be able to share valuable information with your followers to better help them in their efforts. You can use Zoom.com to do the recording.

The beauty of this model is you're attracting interested listeners by GIVING! That's a low threshold your followers have in order to start enjoying what you have to share. From there you're able to present them with ads that complement your niche and give them more helpful ideas to consider with affiliate offers.

As for the people you interview, they may have an affiliate program you can offer links to and generate commissions that way as well (More on that in the section on Podcasting).

By interviewing experts, you too become an authority. This grows over time as you interview more people. This can help generate influence with your listeners and email subscribers, which can translate into more sales as you suggest products and services they may find helpful.

28. LAND INVESTING

Being a third generation real estate investor, my family has always concentrated on houses for the most part, however my grandfather did have a small apartment complex.

In all that time, I don't ever once remember us talking about investing in land. We always thought more about buying a property for the ability to charge rent, generate income, and experience some kind of tax benefit and equity appreciation.

That all changed when I met my friend Jack. He came to this country from Germany in the late 1990's. He told me he didn't speak English well, and he didn't have a lot of money when he first got to the United States. What he did have was a lot of AMBITION and a willingness to search for opportunities that many investors overlooked.

Jack started investing in land, and when I met him around 2007 he'd already done over 2,000 land deals! That in itself is impressive, but what appealed to me most was HOW he was acquiring these properties for pennies on the dollar, FREE AND CLEAR, and turning them into cash or monthly payments. Needless to say this changed his money scenario and he's living proof that the American Dream is alive and well.

Generally speaking, he figured out a way to buy vacant land from "don't-wanter" owners for cash, CHEAP. Considering the land was free and clear to begin with, there were no existing loans to deal with during the negotiating and purchasing process.

Once you own property like this that's located in an area with demand, you can flip it fast at a discount, or sell it on monthly payments for less of a discount and more profit. Depending on what you paid for the land, you may cover your purchase money with the down payment of the buyer making payments. If you do this a few times, you can grow the amount of monthly checks you receive. If you do this a LOT of times, you may have a passive income stream to Stack that makes you very happy!

If you'd like to hear how to do this from Jack himself, you'll find a link to Land Investing on my website PassiveIncomeStacking.com/income-sources.

29. LAUNDROMAT

Many wealthy people establish and grow their net worth by owning successful businesses.

Some start these companies themselves, pouring countless hours and years into them until they produce a nice income.

That can take a lot of start-up capital, overhead, and TIME!

We're looking for PASSIVE processes here, right?

With that goal in mind, first determine if there are areas near where you live that have established laundromats FOR SALE.

If so, get with a seasoned COMMERCIAL real estate broker and have them get all the information that's available to prospective buyers. Have them explain the stated income and expenses. If they seem reasonable and you're interested in proceeding slowly and cautiously, share your findings with your accountant and attorney to get their opinions.

You don't want to buy a company that doesn't have a proven track record. Yes, maybe you can improve the current operations to generate even more cash flow, but you don't want to invest in a business where you're simply taking over someone else's problem that they're more than willing to get rid of (unload).

To make buying this established business even more passive for you, consider hiring someone else to perform the daily duties for you.

Because this is a CASH business, hire someone you trust, and make sure YOU personally oversee things so that money isn't being pocketed without you knowing it.

30. LEAD GENERATION WEBSITE

You've already learned how you can create websites for free using Word-Press.com. By attracting certain "lead type" visitors to your website, you have a chance to capture their contact information in return for some helpful advice or personal contact to help them even more.

These types of leads are helpful to business owners in the niche you're targeting because they aren't cold leads, they're WARM leads who have indicated they're interested and possibly in NEED of the service being offered.

You can take this as far as you'd like, but for this example let's say you're focusing on providing leads to businesses in your area for a fee.

One reason to keep it local is because you can *target* regional, long-tail keyword searches in your SEO (Search Engine Optimization) marketing and paid Google AdWords ads. That simply means you've designed the keywords on your *website* and in your *marketing* to target people doing online searches for things such as "Niche-Business in Your City", instead of just, "Niche-Business". That helps you target your website copy, along with online ads you may choose to place to generate some traffic from your locale.

Which type of businesses do you think might be interested in your lead generation services that would pay you an amount that might make you happy? Are attorneys in your area paying a lot for advertising? Do you see them on billboards, television ads, bus stops, etc.? This type of advertising is not cheap.

Do you think insurance agents would jump at the chance to get out-side leads to help them meet their quota and grow their client base? Do you think real estate brokers that head up certain franchised offices would like more home seller and buyer leads?

You can choose which businesses are willing to pay $5, $10, $20+ per lead. You can outsource the creation of these types of websites in as many niches as you feel would be profitable. Once they're up they can pretty much run on their own 24/7.

31. MEMBERSHIP SITE

Do you know why phone companies advertise so much to get you to switch from your carrier to their service? Do you know why gyms try so hard to get you to sign up? Do you know why razor companies try to get you to commit to pay very little money each month to get a new razor sent to you? CONSISTENT MONTHLY INCOME!

Companies with a monthly continuity component often offer different incentives to get people to not only commit to pay each month, but commit to pay for at least ONE YEAR. They attract us, and then they give us further incentive to commit for a longer period of time where we will CONTINUE to pay our monthly payment or an annual payment at a discount.

The good news is that YOU can offer your own type of membership using your free WordPress.com website by offering EXCLUSIVE content or contact with you for a monthly price.

We've mentioned creating a website in niches where you can generate income in several ways. For those people hungry for more information in your niche, you can offer a membership component by using software such as that found at Wishlistproducts.com. That software can be "plugged-in" to your WordPress.com blog.

You can upload exclusive content only available to paid members that is "dripped" automatically each day, every few days, every week, monthly, you decide. This way your members always know more good content is always around the corner.

You can do live group calls once or twice a month where you share information and take questions. Record the calls to add to your membership area so members can access them going forward. In order to get access, people must pay you a monthly fee or a discounted annual fee so you can generate more money up front.

The more $10, $20, $37, or $97 monthly members you have, the more exciting the monthly income has the potential to become. Grab your calculator and begin to dream a little. (For those that want even more personal assistance, consider charging higher priced one-on-one sessions.)

32. MOBILE HOME PARK INVESTING

As I mentioned earlier in this book, I used to live in a singlewide mobile home for 6 years. That gave me a firsthand glimpse of how my mobile home park was operated.

Since that time, mobile home park investing has become a more popular topic because of several factors.

One is the demand for affordable housing. A mobile home is a way for people to have their own home that they can buy on payments like a vehicle, without owning the land. Because they don't own the land, they pay rent on the lot that the home sits on.

Mobile home park owners can buy cheap mobile homes, put them on lots in their park, and sell the home on payments while charging lot rent. I essentially said the same thing in the last two paragraphs, but from two completely different perspectives.

The homeowner who is making payments is happy because they have a home they feel is their own, even though they often don't own it completely and they don't own the land.

The park owner is happy because they may be doing this with SEVERAL mobile homes. That leads us to another HUGE benefit of mobile home park investing and that's the potential for MASSIVE CASH FLOW!

When you have several people paying you monthly payments to buy a mobile home, along with lot rent, it adds up. Because affordable housing should always be in demand, mobile home park investing is considered by many to be *recession proof.*

During the recession in the early 2000's, investment companies bought up cheap houses to rent. As I write this, that is happening with mobile home parks as well.

The "long game" is investment companies are banking on people needing affordable housing to survive. Mobile home parks are considered affordable, and the demand proves it. If you don't want to own the park, you might consider buying shares in a REIT (Real Estate Investment Trust – more on REITs a little later).

33. PATREON

In this book we've discussed multiple ways to generate income online. Another potential passive income source to consider stacking is DONATIONS. You might wonder why people would voluntarily give their money to people who are giving away free content, but it's a reality happening every day with the help of Patreon.com.

Imagine you've determined the niche or niches you want to create your free WordPress.com website in. You're giving something away for free on your website in exchange for your interested visitors email address. You're sending out a newsletter and making videos or audios on a regular basis.

You're effectively building a relationship with your followers. You're offering affiliate products, advertising, and maybe even some of your own products.

Patreon.com allows you one more way to offer your loyal followers a way to support you. You can ask people to help support your efforts for a monthly donation, or you can UP THEIR EXPERIENCE while you give them a little something extra for an even larger donation.

Often as creators of content, we can get bogged down with the business side of these types of activities. That's where Patreon.com can help you with their ready built platform, support system, and payment processing. You can decide what type of extras you'd like to offer people for their continued extra monthly support. You might even consider this as your tailor made membership site software team.

You may want to offer exclusive trainings to those people who commit to donate a certain amount monthly. Or maybe you'll want to have an exclusive LIVE group video session using Zoom.com once or twice a month to connect with your most dedicated followers. You may consider a higher Patreon monthly donation commitment as a price of entry for a more *personal experience* with you.

You can have different membership tiers, special offers, workshops, merchandise for membership, and more to help generate additional income sources to add to your Stack with Patreon.com.

34. PEER-TO-PEER LENDING

Because loans from banks can be a little more expensive than borrowers would like to pay, and because the interest rates and return on investment offered by banks to investors is often lower than many would like…

Peer-To-Peer lending websites are out there to help create a win-win for both sides of the transaction. One reason this is achievable is because there's no longer a "middleman" which is usually the bank.

If you stop to think about it, the bank is getting their money from depositors. The way to attract depositors is by offering to pay interest on the amount deposited. The bank often then loans that money out to borrowers.

In order for the bank to make money, they need to earn a "spread" on the difference of what they're paying to depositors, and what they're charging borrowers. With peer-to-peer lending, you no longer have a bank in the middle taking *their cut* of the money.

Lendingclub.com is one of the largest P2P sites out there, but you can find more by doing an online search. The types of loans that borrowers are often seeking are…

- Auto Loans
- Business Loans
- Home Loans
- Personal Loans
- Medical Loans (medical expenses not covered by insurance)
- Student Loans
- Student Loan Refinances

If you have extra money that you'd like to get working for you, simply do an online search for "peer to peer lending" and see what's being offered. Make sure to do your due diligence and run it by your CPA and attorney before you start.

35. PHOTOGRAPHY AND VIDEOS

These days most everyone has the chance to be a pretty good photographer and videographer because of the high quality camera that is inside our phones. You've undoubtedly seen a landscape on your travels, pulled out your phone, framed it up and clicked away. Once done you looked at the screen and realized you just might be the next great photographer or cinematographer!

You then opened up the app and chose the filter that made your amazing photo look even more impressive. You hit save with a sense of accomplishment and pride knowing there's *one more thing* that you're good at.

Way to go, if you get a little more conscious and purposeful of your surroundings you just might be able to generate a passive income using websites such as…

Dreamstime.com
Shutterstock.com

Simply sign up for an account, and when people download your photos or videos, YOU get paid. If you live in a unique part of the world, consider taking photos and videos of what makes it unique so people have the chance to pay you for your good-eye.

Some categories to consider supplying photos and videos are…

Architecture – Funny - Nature and landscapes - Jobs and careers – Costume themes - Pets and animals - Science and technology - Seasonal and holiday - Fitness and wellness - Fashion and beauty – Hobbies – Food - Sports and recreation - Travel destinations – Action, etc.

Go to the websites above and see what's available and the categories that are represented. As long as it's clean, fun, and in good taste, you'll most likely find it there. Determine the categories and keyword phrases that work best for the photos and videos you like to take, and you're on your way.

36. PODCAST

These days anybody can throw their hat into the podcasting game. The good news is there are plenty of people out there willing and able to listen while they're working out, commuting, making dinner, doing chores or just relaxing. People are actively open to learning new things, especially those that they're interested in and passionate about.

First do an online search for podcasts in the categories you might like to focus on. See what others are talking about in your niche and take notes of the things you like best about each. Begin crafting a platform, show theme, and brand that gets you excited because when you're excited, others can hear that in your voice which helps make your show more enjoyable to listen to.

You can have solo-episodes where it's just you talking about different topics within your niche. You can also include interviews where you ask people questions that have some kind of authority or expertise in your niche that your listeners would benefit from. It takes effort and time to create your episodes, but once set up online they're ready for people to enjoy 24/7.

Your podcast isn't just about entertainment, it's also a tool used like a magnet to help pull in viewers and subscribers. You can also have a website dedicated to your podcast that includes all kinds of ways to help make it a money generator.

We've gone over different ways to create income from a WordPress. com website of your own. This is similar except your podcast is also plugged into it. You can still be offering something for free to get visitors to sign up for your email list. On your personal podcast website you can include your products, affiliate products, advertising, webinar broadcast pages, etc.

For each individual podcast episode you create, you can have an independent "Show Notes" page with more content on the subject being covered, along with monetized affiliate links and more advertising. Be sure to disclose when you are using affiliate links based on the guidelines set by the Federal Trade Commission (FTC). As your podcast listenership grows, so should your authority and opportunities to earn more income.

37. PRIVATE MONEY BROKER

There are a couple ways to potentially profit being a private money broker. First, let's dissect this to give you a better perspective of the two sides of this type of transaction and how you can benefit on either end. Real estate investors often find themselves in the need for money to do their deals, either to initially acquire a property and/or gather funds for rehab and fix-up. An active real estate investor could have a lot of deals going on at the same time and be routinely making money on a regular basis, but they often find themselves strapped for cash because all of their money is tied up in the deals they currently have in progress. Unless they have a very good relationship with a bank (which is rare), they most likely can't use this type of traditional lending institution because the qualification requirements are plentiful, the costs of the money are high, and it takes too long for the money to become available.

Another money option for the active investor is to go to a Hard Money Lender. They can fund money to investors quickly, but it's EXPENSIVE. It can be a viable option if the money is only needed for a short period of time, as long as there's enough profit in the deal to warrant it.

Another *more affordable* option is having a private lender available to borrow money from quickly and at a better rate than many hard money lenders are willing to offer. The challenge for some investors is knowing how to find good private money lenders in an appropriate and lawful way. That's where having a private money broker is absolutely vital to their business…and now YOU can make a nice fee income by being the broker, that vital conduit between real estate investors and private money lenders. Imagine getting paid $1,000-$10,000 just for helping deserving people get the funding they desperately need to be a success in real estate.

Lucky for you, I know someone who has a company that specializes in attracting private money lenders. He even allows people to earn fees by BROKERING this private money supply. It's a simple to follow process to make money by helping others get the funding they need to invest in real estate. If you'd like to learn how to set this viable business model up and start earning fee income checks – visit PassiveIncomeStacking.com/income-sources.

38. PRODUCT DESIGN

CafePress.com and Redbubble.com are websites where you can upload your personal artwork for people to buy to put on t-shirts, mugs, pillows, posters, stickers and more.

If you've got artistic ability, this can be a fun outlet for your creative side to earn some cash.

Once your designs are up on the website, people can choose to buy them. It will obviously take you some effort to initially create your masterpieces, but once available for purchase they have the chance to generate revenue for years to come.

Consider this your *permanent online gallery* available for purchase.

Take a look at the websites mentioned above and see which items jump off the page. Notice what makes them do that so you can begin positioning your creations to better appeal to the browsers looking for things to buy.

Think themes, colors, topics, interests, humor, quotes, current events, pop-culture, pet breeds, large local areas with loyal residents, favorite foods, hobbies, etc.

Look at Google Images for ideas that you like, and then create something uniquely yours.

If you enjoy drawing, or creating art using software, this will hopefully be a fun project that you might enjoy doing even if you weren't trying to get paid. Like they say, if you like what you're doing it's not work.

Create social pages like Pinterest, Instagram, Facebook and Twitter to get the message out by sharing some of your fun designs.

Offer something for free in exchange for an email address so you can begin to alert people when you have new items available. You might even consider a Patreon.com account to drum up more financial support as you're working hard on your projects.

39. PRODUCT FUNNEL

If you decide to create online income, one way to automate potential sales coming in is with an email product funnel.

The good news is you don't have to have any of your own products to do this with. You can set this up with OTHER people's products and offer them as an affiliate. If you later decide to create your own products, you can have a product funnel for them as well. Or, you can have a funnel with both other people's products and your own.

You can first create a free website using WordPress.com. Next create something to give away for free such as a report, video, blueprint, etc. Offer this on your website for free in exchange for your visitors email address. This is how they get into your email *funnel* to begin with.

A funnel is merely an analogy for an *email sequence* that is dripped out over time. You accomplish this with an email autoresponder. These are emails you set up to go out on specific days at specific times.

For example, let's say someone goes to your website today and "opts-in" to receive your freebie by supplying their email address. Your email autoresponder would have an email that goes out immediately that gives them what they are expecting to get (very important), and a welcome into your "family" with other supporting copy to begin the relationship and engagement.

Your next email might be set up in advance to go out on day 2 at 2:00 p.m. Eastern Time. It might include some content in your niche to better solidify the fact that you send emails with VALUE. Keep doing that every 2-3 days for a week or so and THEN start including monetized offers that you will get paid for when people buy.

If you're offering affiliate products, once your subscriber clicks/taps an affiliate link inside your email, if they buy, their purchase is tracked back to you so you get paid a commission. You can set up emails in your product funnel email autoresponder to go out every few days for weeks, months, or even years. It takes effort to set up, but it's passive from then on.

40. PRODUCT LAUNCH

If you're on email lists of people that sell products, chances are you've been sent emails that are part of a *product launch*. The reason for sending these emails is simple because they are valuable, effective, and potentially VERY PROFITABLE for those sending them. Let's break it down a bit because it's both an art and science. To begin with, there is a definite time frame that a product launch is designed within. There are different models, so let's go over two for you to consider.

Longer Product Launch:

One hypothetical example is having some teaching videos that go live on Day 1, Day 3, and Day 5. Nothing is sold in these emails. They're designed to peek interest and push people to the video pages. On the video pages is also usually a way for people to get more information by providing their email address. This gets them officially "opted-in" to the product launch FUNNEL directly from the source. The videos are designed to be informative but incomplete. They offer *value* to the viewer as they teach something, peek their interest, and get them conditioned to *want* to learn more. They can do that when the next video becomes live.

Let's say Day 7 is when the product sales page goes LIVE <u>and</u> webinars with the FULL story become available for viewing. Let's also say the offer will be live for the next 5 days only. It's at this beginning point when the people behind the scenes of the actual product being offered monitor sales. Chances are things won't go as planned so the tweaking of webinar content, sales copy and email copy begins.

There MUST be a HARD DEADLINE when sales will no longer be processed to get people to act and buy. It's during the time between when the sales page and webinar goes live - and the deadline - that email marketers PUSH the emails. If the promotion is a success, sales usually come on Day 1, the middle day of the promotion, and the day the offer shuts down. The hard deadline forces people to buy, generating more sales.

A Shorter Product Launch/Offer goes without the free videos in the beginning and simply sends people to a sales page or webinar registration page. The offer lasts 3-4 days with the majority of sales happening on the last day, again because of the hard deadline and close down of the offer.

41. REAL ESTATE CROWDFUNDING

If you like the idea of real estate investing, it's fun to think of the different and unique ways you may choose to invest. Of course there's the traditional way of investing in real estate by actually buying the property, be it residential or commercial.

But if you have the money and you'd like to invest some of your capital into different commercial real estate opportunities without doing all the heavy lifting, Real Estate Crowdfunding is something you may want to investigate further.

Many real estate crowdfunding websites will most likely only deal with accredited investors proving they have ample income and savings. You may find some that overlook those criteria.

(If you're concerned about having enough money to become accredited, don't worry we'll be covering REITs soon which is another way to take advantage of commercial property with less money).

Real Estate Crowdfunding offers you the ability to find projects and scenarios needing capital. Unlike REITs that include a number of different real estate properties and investments, with crowdfunding you're usually investing in a specific property or investment focus.

This is an important distinction because it gives you the ability to choose locations and property types to best fit your objectives and preferences.

With so many Real Estate Crowdfunding companies in existence today, always do your due diligence to first pick the best companies to consider working with, and then for the projects you think may have potential.

Because these are larger deals, there's more to lose in case your investment goes south. Because of that always consult with your attorney and accountant before investing so you have professionals to guide you in this process.

42. REAL ESTATE WEBSITES

Because I focus a lot on real estate and have created several products on the subject over the years, I've come to find many unique ways to potentially profit with it that I share with my subscribers.

One passive way to create a foundation for real estate activity is with websites that are strategically designed for certain types of real estate, and the investors who focus their business around them.

You can choose to attack this in a couple different ways…

1. Have a website designed to attract motivated home sellers – this helps you uncover bargain house leads.

2. Have a website designed to attract motivated commercial property sellers – this helps you uncover bargain commercial property leads.

You have some choices when it comes to your desired method of harvesting these leads…

A) You can buy the properties for your own portfolio and rent them out.

B) You can buy the properties at a deep enough discount to sell them for a quick pay day to a retail or wholesale buyer.

C) You can sell the "purchase contract" to an investor.

D) You can sell the "leads" to investors.

The great part is once you have your websites set up, they can work FOR YOU 24/7. You'll find turn-key websites available and ready for you to plug-in on my website PassiveIncomeStacking.com/income-sources.

43. REITS

If you want to invest in real estate but don't have the time, the confidence, or the current knowledge to start, REITs may be something to consider.

REIT is an acronym for Real Estate Investment Trust.

Think of them kind of like a mutual fund that owns a number of different real estate assets. You can buy shares of REITs on stock exchanges.

The two main types of REITs are focused on "equity". In the portfolios held inside these types of REITs are properties owned for the long-term. Money is earned inside these REITs through the rent these properties generate, along with the equity build up and sale of these properties.

Another type is a "mortgage" REIT known as an mREIT. In the portfolios held inside these types of mREITs are mortgages (debts secured by real estate) or mortgage securities. These types of mortgages can be tied to commercial real estate, residential properties, or both.

Another benefit of owning REITs are the DIVIDENDS one can earn. As we mentioned earlier in the dividend section, dividends are payments made by companies to its shareholders. It's a way for those who own REIT shares to realize some of the profits in the portfolio, up and above an increase in the price per share of the REIT.

Let's say the real estate market is hot and rental prices on apartments are very expensive. Buying an apartment building may be out of your reach, but buying more affordable shares of a REIT of your choice may offer you the amount of investment exposure you're looking for without keeping you up at night.

Or maybe you want to take advantage of all the demand for Long Term Care facilities, Retirement Homes, Memory Care establishments, etc. You can find REITs that offer you that kind of investment as well. For more good information on REITs visit REIT.com.

44. RENT ADVERTISING SPACE ON YOUR CAR

Finally, a way to help make your Lamborghini payment!

Do you drive a lot of miles each week? Do you commute long distances for work? Do you provide Uber or Lyft type rides? Would you like a little happier way of feeling about all the hours you spend in your car and away from the people and activities that mean the most to you?

If you answered YES…then Carvertise.com and Wrapify.com may be something to consider.

You can check out their criteria, but basically you need to drive a minimum amount of miles, and have a car that isn't too old.

Once you sign up, you can pick the advertising you're willing to have on your car. There will most likely be a number of brands you may already be familiar with to choose from. Fortune 500 companies utilize these types of advertising services along with new companies trying to get some exposure.

When you agree to an ad, it will be applied to your car in the form of "wraps". You've undoubtedly seen company vehicles driving around your area with all kinds of graphics on them. Those are applied with a vinyl type decal that goes over your car's paint. You should have the choice of a "partial" or "full" wrap.

There should be a certain amount of time that you're willing to commit having the wrap on your car so the advertiser gets their share of views.

You may also have to prove the amount of miles you've driven to satisfy the commitment made between you and the advertiser. Sometimes the longer you commute, the more you may be paid.

45. RENT YOUR EQUIPMENT

Do you have a lot of expensive equipment lying around? If people need to use a piece of expensive equipment only once, they're more willing to rent it for the day or week.

Another reason why people may be willing to rent equipment instead of purchasing it is because they simply don't have the space to keep it. For those living in an apartment, space is limited for even the most basic items.

You might do some research to see what kind of items are currently being offered for rent in your area that have DEMAND. If you think you can acquire the same items affordably, then turn around and rent them for *less* than the competition, you may be on to something.

Some items to consider renting might be…

Appliances, arcade games, audio equipment, party supplies, bounce house, popcorn machine, dumpsters, camping supplies, lawn maintenance supplies, specialized tools and equipment, formal wear and costumes, multimedia projector, wedding supplies, canoe rental, log splitter, snow blower, chocolate fountain, etc.

When people have a NEED for some of these kinds of things, it's for a specific reason within a specific amount of time. That means the decision becomes EMOTIONAL. They really want these things because they have a very good reason for wanting them. But there's only one problem, they don't own these things and they either CAN'T or WON'T buy them.

That's when your service becomes of GREAT VALUE to them!

Make sure to do a deep dive into the *successful competition* in your area. Once you have that information, create a service that's BETTER and MORE AFFORDABLE and see what other things within your niche may have demand that you can capitalize on.

46. RENTAL PROPERTY

Real estate is one way an average person can potentially get ahead, IF they make good decisions in the process. Just buying a property doesn't mean you're on the path to wealth. If you buy the wrong property, at the wrong price, in the wrong location, or at the wrong time, you will most likely lose money. On the other hand, if you use free websites like Zillow. com to gain some market knowledge, you'll be able to learn a lot of things not available to investors before the Internet. Add to that knowledge by getting good advice from a few seasoned real estate agents and your due diligence is well on its way.

I've had rental houses that I've managed myself, and I also used to manage my parents rental houses. I'd find tenants, collect rents, schedule repairs, make the mortgage payments, you name it. Actively managing real estate can be less than passive if you're buying the type of properties that require higher maintenance, higher management, and suffer from a lot of turnover. So for starters I'd suggest staying away from those kind of properties.

We always bought NICE affordable houses in areas people liked living in. That meant there was DEMAND, and the chance to attract tenants with better credit and a more solid payment history.

When I rent out property I offer it with a $50 rent incentive. The tenants receive a $50 discount on rent each month if they pay BEFORE the 1st of the month, AND take care of any minor maintenance needs up to $50 per month. What that creates is a grateful tenant who has the chance to SAVE up to $600 a year if they merely pay before the first, and DON"T bother me with little maintenance issues like a clogged toilet.

I let them know that I want the place to be in good working order and not to let things go unfixed just to save $50. I ask them to tell me when bigger things need attention so I can have them fixed quickly. I don't do the repairs myself as that's out of my skill set. When I know there's work to be done, as much as I don't like the expense, I know it's just a "phone call and a check" and it's fixed. When the income warrants it you might consider hiring a property management company to handle things to free up your time even more so you can look for more rental properties. You can determine if you want to invest in condos/townhouses, houses, duplexes, four-plexes, or apartments.

47. RENT OUT STORAGE SPACE

I had a property once near the Arizona Cardinals football team's stadium. Besides the regular NFL games that were played there, other large events used the facility such as the college football Fiesta Bowl, and two Super Bowls.

When it came time for the Super Bowl, because the property I had was so close to the stadium, home owners were targets for special kinds of marketing. It was probably about two months before the Super Bowl that I first started seeing signs staked into the ground with ads like, "Rent Out Your House During The Super Bowl for $10,000!".

Can you imagine seeing a sign like that as you're driving into your neighborhood? I didn't take them up on that, but it did get me thinking about alternatives. Considering the amount of people that visit a city during a Super Bowl, it really is like one of the world's biggest parties for about a week. Would people with RV's be open to paying for space near the stadium for a few days?

Let's switch gears. If you have land that's in an area where people have things they need to store, you might be able to rent that area out for serious passive income. Because I live in Arizona where a lot of people have toys to help them enjoy recreational activities, there are 2 big demands for storage space – boats and RV's. Your area may have other types of large toys in need of storage.

Because Phoenix is the 5th largest metropolitan area in the country, we also have a lot of semi-trucks importing and exporting goods. In one city locally, there is a road where many truck drivers would park overnight and sleep. You'd see so many trucks parked on both sides of the street at night that the city came in and put up "No Parking" signs.

That's a great example of DEMAND. Do you think those truck drivers would have loved an alternative place to park and sleep undisturbed at night? Do you think they'd be willing to pay some money to SECURE their spot? If you have land that's zoned accordingly, consider what other types of storage demands are out there in your area and consider offering a solution for a fee.

48. REVIEW WEBSITE

I remember years ago one time being on a group mastermind call with some very accomplished people. The topic of our discussion was completely unrelated, but as the call was wrapping up and people were jumping off, for some reason this one person and I started a conversation between the two of us.

He told me about something else he was doing and having a lot of success with. He said he would share the details, but at the time asked me not to divulge the niche to anybody as to not increase his competition. With that understood he went on to tell me what he was doing and that was creating Review Websites. I was already impressed with what he was sharing, but when he said he was making *monthly* what some people make *annually*, it really got my attention.

As originally promised I can't share the niche, but I can give you some overview details for you to decide if it's something that interests you. Like the name implies, you're offering online reviews of certain products, software, etc. in hopes it helps people looking for more information to make a good buying decision.

Your goal with this is to get TRAFFIC, and a lot of it to your website. That's where good Search Engine Optimization (SEO) comes in. One way to help with this is to use a lot of keywords that are specific to what you're reviewing. Really niche it down so when the main search engines process your website, it's apparent to the algorithms being used that you're offering a lot of VALUE to the person searching for things in your niche.

You're attracting interested people with your reviews. You're monetizing your website with affiliate links to the products you're talking about. When someone clicks your link and then buys that product, you get paid a commission. To help create a larger potential income with this strategy, consider reviewing higher priced products that have a lot of demand and online searches. See what competitors are doing in the niches you're considering so you can provide an even better review service.

TheWireCutter.com is a good example of a review website. To help make this even more fun, consider products to review within some of the hobbies and things you're passionate about, assuming there's demand of course.

49. ROTH IRA AND ROTH 401K

So far this book has been dedicated to growing your money. We've discussed a lot of different strategies to consider. There's one HUGE component to all of this that we haven't really mentioned. When it comes to your finances, income, business efforts, investments, and profits, you have a partner and they want to take a lot of your hard earned income. By the way, we all have this partner so you're not alone in this. It's the Government!

The taxes we pay is our partner's "cut", and if we aren't careful they will take a LOT more than we would like. If you think about it, we're taxed when we make money – we're taxed when we spend money – and if we work hard, take risks, and sacrifice greatly to make more money, we are put into a HIGHER tax bracket so we pay even more taxes. Finally, if we've been able to save up a boat load of money after all the years our "partner" has taken their cut, the money we leave to our heirs, if the amount is high enough, will get taxed too.

Our partner does offer us SOME ways to keep a little more of our hard earned money. Two of those ways are with a ROTH IRA (Individual Retirement Account) and ROTH 401K. I'm not giving tax advice here, and the rules can change as all things seem to do.

Both of these instruments allow you to put AFTER TAX dollars into these types of savings accounts. These are dollars you earned and paid taxes on. Once the funds are in these accounts, you don't have to pay any *capital gains tax* on the EXTRA money that's generated inside these accounts. If you have stocks, index funds, REITs, mutual funds, etc. inside these accounts and they go up in value, when you cash them out you won't have to pay taxes on your gains.

Remember the "Rule Of 72" conversation earlier about how your money compounds? These types of accounts will help you KEEP more of what you earned. There are limits to how much you can contribute to these accounts. In regards to Passive Income Stacking™, a portion of the money you generate with Macro Category 1 could go into this type of Macro Category 2 investment account. Do an online search for more of the current specifics, and talk to your CPA and investment advisor to learn how to best take advantage of a ROTH IRA and ROTH 401K within your own portfolio.

50. STORAGE UNITS

Do you remember when you started this book and I shared one of the things my father used to say to me all the time? It was, "We need more cash flow!" The goal of owning storage units is all about the cash flow you can generate, and how you can maximize and grow it.

We are a consumer driven economy. Credit is rampant, and people love to shop and collect things that go down in value that they really don't need. We also have a hard time getting rid of our STUFF. That's probably because it's OUR stuff, and we paid good money for it. So there's NO WAY we're getting rid of it. When we move we take our boxes of stuff with us. Forget the fact that we may not have looked inside the boxes since the last time we moved. That doesn't stop us from the joyful activity of shopping and collecting more stuff to the point when we no longer have space for it. Instead of getting rid of it, we find a place that charges RENT where we can STORE our stuff. Gotta love it!

So the need and demand for *storage units* is alive and well. The cash flow opportunity becomes that much more attractive when you consider storage facilities don't have many of the hassles associated with owning and renting houses or apartments.

Plus there's the diversification. For example, if you have one rental house and the tenant stops paying rent, you're not getting paid that month. But with a storage facility that has a lot of units, if some people don't pay, you're still getting money from the other renters.

There are right and wrong ways to approach this business. The people who get it right and purchase or build by following a winning plan have a chance for success. Those that don't can experience a very costly mistake to say the least. The latter are the people that sell for pennies on the dollar to investors who know the correct steps to take.

51. TAX ABATEMENT

We've talked before how the government taxes us in many ways. Not the least of which is property tax. If you own a house during times of inflation or high demand, the value of your house has most likely appreciated, meaning its gone up in value. The county tax assessor is well aware of this fact, so over time your property taxes go up as well.

When the real estate market later changes and goes down, your property tax should go down as well, eventually. If you aren't satisfied with the amount of property tax you're being charged because you think it's too high, you could always consider contacting the county tax assessor's office and see if they'll reduce it.

With that understanding in place, can you imagine how much more this is multiplied when dealing with larger commercial real estate? The owners of this kind of property are most likely concentrating on other business activities. They may have NO IDEA they are paying more property tax that they should or could be.

If you were to get educated on how your local county tax assessor calculates property tax assessments, you can then begin to determine if the CURRENT property tax being charged to commercial building owners is high, low, or about right. Real estate markets fluctuate. That means the appropriate property tax that SHOULD be charged should fluctuate some as well. Many times as property owners we KNOW there will be property tax that will be owed, so we accept the amount the tax assessor charges.

Once you understand market conditions, how to determine the assessor's criteria and calculations, you can begin to uncover how certain commercial property types in your area are taxed. Owners will usually always have to pay property tax, but your goal for them is to get theirs reduced, while you receive a *percentage of the reduction.*

If you find a sector of the commercial market that seems to be over-charged, you can reach out to several owners and try to get that corrected for a percentage of the reduction. You might calculate the savings based on a 10 year period so it's more substantial. Your percentage might be derived from this higher number. Do some research on how to best structure this, and what stage the real estate market is in.

52. TAX CERTIFICATES AND TAX DEEDS

What happens when a property owner DOES NOT pay their property taxes? The county government tries to enforce payment to the point where the property owner can and will lose their property.

There are two main ways counties across the United States enforce the payment of delinquent property tax – Tax Certificates and Tax Deeds. These are two DIFFERENT things, and states usually choose one of these methods.

First you need to determine which of these methods (or both) that you might like to profit with. Next you need to find out which states collect delinquent property taxes the way you would like to participate as an investor.

The reason why Tax Lien Certificates are attractive is because of the higher than usual interest being offered. Within tax certificate states, the county offers a tax lien certificate to bidders willing to pay the outstanding tax amount owed. Depending on location, the interest being offered to investors is up to 16% or higher.

When counties offer tax lien certificates, they START the bidding with an interest rate they are willing to pay to an investor. Investors then bid the interest rate DOWN. The bidding has ended when the county is left with the investor willing to take the LEAST amount of interest on the tax lien certificate. The investor then pays the amount owed to the county in delinquent taxes. If the property owner eventually pays the back taxes within a set amount of time, the investor gets their original money back plus the interest agreed to by the county. If the property owner does not pay the back taxes, the investor gets the property. In most cases, the property owner pays the back taxes.

As for Tax Deed States, there is usually no interest paid on the deed because you're actually bidding on the tax delinquent property you want to *buy out right*. When the county offers homes for sale through tax auctions, the highest bidder gets the property. Your goal is to get the property at a deep discount. If you'd like to learn how to set up both of these types of income streams for your Stack visit... PassiveIncomeStacking.com/income-sources.

53. TAX FORECLOSURE OVERAGES

When people buy houses, they often get a loan that's insured by the government. These would be FHA loans and VA loans.

When people default on the loan and stop making payments, the government forecloses on the home and becomes the new owner. The government then turns around and sells the property to the highest bidder to recoup the money owed.

On average, thousands of Property Tax Foreclosure Auctions are happening all over the United States each business day. Any EXTRA money generated from the sale of the property owner's home to pay back the property taxes - that's left over - is actually owed to the original owner of the property. This money is referred to as an OVERAGE.

The original property owner will only get paid this money if they're aware of this money and THEY ASK FOR IT. Those are two details that property owners rarely know. Because they aren't aware of these things THEY DON'T ASK FOR THE MONEY THEY ARE OWED. That's where you come in to help these people get some of this money that they would otherwise never see, for a *Finder's Fee*.

You can generate as much as 30% - 40% Finder's Fees for helping the original property owner get their piece of the "overage" that was paid on their property at the tax foreclosure auction. You would be providing a very helpful service because this money would probably help these people greatly as chances are they may still be struggling financially. This service you would be providing them would be a true win-win arrangement.

An attractive aspect of this is you don't need money to invest. You're just learning how to access the list of people owed the money and some other pertinent aspects to run this and you can be on your way.

If you'd like to learn how to set this business model up and start earning finder's fees – visit PassiveIncomeStacking.com/income-sources.

54. VENDING MACHINES

I once owned used book stores in the Phoenix area. They were fun for people to visit because they had all kinds of collectibles and memorabilia on the walls and hanging from above the aisles, and we had a juke box that played nostalgic hits.

We used to get visited by vendors offering to put displays inside with merchandise. When an item was sold, we would each get a slice of the profits. It was easy for my business because all we did was track sales. The VENDOR did everything else. That's the business model for *vending machines*, except YOU are the vendor. First research businesses in your area to see if there's a viable market to try to tap into.

Second you need to find vending machines you can afford. If you can fix things, nice used machines may work. Do an online search for "vending machines" to start your due diligence. Vending.com is a service that offers different types of new vending machines such as factory direct Combo, Snack, and Drink vending machines, and they offer FINANC-ING.

Start small so you don't over extend yourself. Make sure there's a demand. Be willing to hear businesses say NO. That's just part of the game. Target businesses that have over 100 employees in the building each day.

Crunch the numbers and see what the break-even point is so you know how much more you must make to get to your desired profit level. Determine how many establishments it will take to have your vending machines in, making a certain amount of PROFIT each, to reach your financial goal.

Reverse engineer your goal into a multi-step plan so that you know how much you can spend on overhead, and how much your machines MUST generate. Once your machine is placed and offering popular items,

ASK what else the people WANT. You might consider a form with a pen you put on the machine itself asking, "What Items Would You Like To See Inside Here So We Can Make You Even Happier?"

To keep this more passive once the machines are placed, if your income warrants it, hire someone else to keep them stocked and maintained.

55. YOUTUBE CHANNEL

We've covered a number of ways to make money online in this book. Many of them can be used together to help with your Passive Income Stacking™. Consider YouTube as one more piece of the bigger puzzle. Yes you can potentially make money having a stand-alone YouTube channel. The criteria to get paid changes based on Google's requirements, as they own YouTube as I write this. Generally speaking you must have a certain amount of subscribers to your channel, and a certain amount of hours of watch-time for your videos per year BEFORE you have the chance to get paid via the ads that appear alongside your videos - Google AdSense Ads.

In order to have the *chance* of generating AdSense Ad revenue, within your YouTube account enable *monetization*, and connect your channel to your AdSense account. Simply do an online search for "Google AdSense" to set up a free account.

If you were to only have a YouTube channel without it being connected to any bigger business model, you would need to get creative to build your audience, get them to become subscribers, and then supply them with a *daily video* to add up the watch-time hours and potential income. I personally like to use YouTube as a tool to get a business message out FOR FREE! People LOVE watching videos. If you have a free WordPress.com website that offers any of the things we've touched on in this book, having a YouTube channel to help support that business model may be helpful. Because you can put YouTube videos on your website, they can help you make a connection with your viewer, along with create engagement and an online relationship with your visitors, customers, and subscribers. This helps bring your website to life.

People do business with those that they feel they know, like and trust. YouTube videos help you achieve this. At the beginning of your YouTube video's written DESCRIPTION you can include a link to your free offer, website, or anything else you like. Have your description start with a link because your video may appear in Google searches as well, and you want people to have YOUR LINK front and center when they find you as they're doing organic keyword searches on Google.

If all these things help you gain enough popularity to make money with your YouTube channel, that's just one more passive income source to add to your Stack!

PART 3

PASSIVE INCOME STACKING™ PREPARING FOR SUCCESS

THE SIMPLE STRATEGY TO HELP ROCK YOUR MARKETING

Once you start having income sources set up, particularly in Passive Macro Category 1 - Money Creation, you may find the need for EXPOSURE to help them build momentum. There are several marketing choices to consider, some more expensive than others. I always like to find affordable and free ways to help market the things I'm doing. It's fun to get creative and think "outside of the box" when it comes to capturing people's imagination with marketing.

Let me share a story with you about a unique marketing campaign I did...

Back in the 1990's when I lived in the mobile home, my family had a used bookstore. It didn't make a lot of money, but it was one of the things we did to generate income at the time. My dad had a whiteboard in the front window that he would write funny, self-deprecating things on to get people's attention. One thing he wrote back then was, "Be Smart Like Us - Reed a Book!" He misspelled "Read" on purpose.

That gave me an idea. Back then Jay Leno used to have a segment on The Tonight Show on Monday's called, "Headlines". With that in mind I placed a 1/3 page ad in our local Penny Saver type newspaper for around $200 that said, "Be Smart Like Us - Reed a Book!" with our store's name, address, phone number, and a map to the store.

Once it came out I sent it to Jay Leno's staff with a letter as if it was coming from a 3rd party saying, "You know how smart bookstores think they are...and this one can't even spell 'Read'!

Within 9 days of sending that ad to The Tonight Show staff it appeared on Jay Leno's desk on Monday's episode. I was floored! Even though it was mentioned on The Tonight Show with millions of viewers, I felt that my customers and most of the people in my area probably weren't as aware of it as I'd have liked.

I had an OPPORTUNITY. In other words, I had something of interest to MARKET!

I wrote a press release to our state's largest newspaper telling the story of what I'd done...the ad, the misspelling, writing to Jay's people, etc. They loved it and did a full story.

I then packaged a copy of the newspaper article along with an updated press release and sent it to ALL of our local TV stations telling them about the story. They loved it too and did LIVE broadcasts from the store talking about the story.

I knew the dates and times the TV stations were coming out and marketed that inside our bookstore letting all our customers know they could come to our "TV Party" where there would be food and drinks, and to tell their friends to watch for them on TV at our store. We had 3 TV stations come out and I milked that story to get a lot more press for our business long after that.

Here's the big take away - whenever you have an income source that has a "unique selling proposition" that HELPS PEOPLE or can POSSITIVELY IMPACT PEOPLE, you have something to MARKET about!

Let me give you a different example of this marketing philosophy to help bring more clarity to this with a different type of business I've also had over the years, real estate investing.

Let's say you invest in real estate. How can you use this marketing strategy within that type of business? First of all, every time you've bought, sold, or rented a house in an area you've HELPED a family, right? That's something to MARKET. Let the ENTIRE NEIGHBORHOOD KNOW that you've *helped another family* and are ready to help them too. That one simple act can potentially springboard 1 deal into more deals. Do that each time you've bought, sold, or rented a house in an area and see what happens over time.

When you've done any kind of real estate deal, you've got something to MARKET. HOW you market the fact that you did that deal AND HELPED PEOPLE in the process can potentially help you generate more business. Plant the seed that YOU are that area's go-to person and keep doing it in areas that you're doing business in so you can prove it.

The Moral – As you set up your MONEY GENERATING passive income sources within your Stack, if *exposure* will help your efforts, look for ways to market the things you're doing by focusing on the BENEFITS they provide. Just so you know where the real power with this is, the magnetism begins with the *benefits*, not necessarily the *facts*.

There are 2 foundational components of marketing – *features* and *benefits*. We learn from the features or facts, but we potentially become emotionally attracted to an offer or service when we hear the benefits it can provide us. Those benefits help *attract* us. Stories inside your marketing that include these benefits are GREAT too.

There's a marketing saying, "Facts tell, Stories sell." I wanted to share these things with you to help give you a better chance for success as you're positioning the message you share with the world about some of the income-generators inside your Stack.

ESTATE PLANNING 101

Let me first start by saying I'm not an attorney or accountant, and I'm not giving any legal, accounting, or investing advice. Always consult a good attorney, accountant, financial planner, and estate planner BEFORE setting up the kind of things I'll be mentioning below.

I just want to share some important essentials to laying the foundation for a strong financial base as you move forward to help grow your empire and legacy for future generations in your family.

Many people think estate planning is done in preparation for when we pass away. That is indeed a part of it, however your "estate" exists NOW, and at all times during your life. It's merely what you own, how you own it, how you protect it, and what you want it to do once your life comes to an end.

Put another way, it's how you RESPONSIBLY set up your life. It's part of the equation of feeling financially SECURE. With this in mind, let's go over a few things to consider.

REVOKABLE LIVING TRUST – With this you can set up your estate to help avoid "Probate" which can be quite costly to your heirs when it's time to liquidate your possessions and money. Within this popular estate planning tool you'll designate who gets what items you own. The "revocable" aspect means you can edit the Trust after it's been originated, and the "living" aspect means you're creating the trust during your lifetime.

LIMITED LIABILITY COMPANY (LLC) – As you're establishing your mini-empire, there may be instances with your money creation efforts when you want to protect yourself from personal liability from your company's liabilities and debts. LLC's are available in the United States. If you're reading this in another country you may want to see what corporate structures like this may be available.

20 YEAR TERM LIFE INSURANCE – To give full credit to this suggestion, I read about this in Dave Ramsey's terrific book, "The Total Money Makeover". When I contacted my longtime friend and insurance agent about this type of coverage his first response was that this is a gift you give to provide for those you love. It's cheaper when you're younger, but if you haven't created a large nest egg *yet*, it's a way to set those up that you care about with a sizeable amount of money once you pass away.

This money can help pay off a house, debts, and just live a more comfortable life. When I originally set up my account I learned that I could have more than one beneficiary, set percentage amounts on each, and change beneficiaries should I ever choose to do so. I mention this to help you if you decide to consider this type of insurance.

PLENTY OF CAR INSURANCE – Even when I had little money, I always tried to have plenty of car insurance, particularly that which covered liability. As I generated and kept more money, that became even more important.

UMBRELLA INSURANCE POLICY – Umbrella insurance provides you with EXTRA liability insurance, up and above what you have on your car, boat, and home. It helps provide extra security for people who may be sued for property damage or personal injuries. When considering premiums, I've found there to be only a small increase when going from

$1 million in coverage to $2 million in coverage with certain companies. It's something to investigate should you consider this type of coverage.

GOOD HEALTH INSURANCE – Medical debts can have a devastating effect on individuals carrying too little health insurance, or for those that have none at all. It can be a quick way to have your life savings wiped out. You worked hard for your money, don't let the lack of appropriate health insurance be the reason you went from Rolls Royce to Skate Board. A silly analogy, but one I'm hoping will make an impression should you ever be tempted to go without enough good health insurance.

LONG TEARM CARE INSURANCE – As we age and need assisted living, the costs of living in such establishments is very expensive. The services vary with the individual's needs, from basic living, memory care, to more specialized continual attention. The costs go up as more services are needed. Having good long term care insurance is a way we can better prepare for our later years from both a monetary stand point, as well as a responsible way to help our family and friend's best care for us.

ROTH IRA, ROTH 401K – We've covered this earlier in the book. It's rare when the U.S. government creates simple ways for individuals to save potentially large amounts of money on taxes. A ROTH IRA (Individual Retirement Account) is something we can create on our own at places like TDAmeritrade.com and Schwab.com. A ROTH 401K can be established at the same places and others, however funded by our companies.

The "Estate Planning 101" list above is just scratching the surface of our estate needs, but it's a pretty good start and one that should be common knowledge to anyone preparing for their best future life. As I stated before, always consult a good attorney, accountant, financial planner, and estate planner BEFORE setting up these kind of things.

LIVING HEALTHY TO ENJOY
YOUR SUCCESS LONGER

To be clear, I'm not a doctor and I'm not giving any health advice here. Always consult a doctor before you choose diets or exercise programs so you know you're getting good professional advice because we only want what's best for you, right?

Have you ever heard about people who work their whole life, retire from their job, and then pass away soon after? I'm not sure why it happens, but I'm determined to keep it from happening to us.

When you have *producing* passive income sources that are Stacked, there's no "job" to retire from. If you create income doing things that give you some kind of joy, you can continue the process until your last day if you like. Another side benefit is it will give you something to do, that you can take pride in that provides you and your family the needed funds to potentially spend your "retired" years in style doing the things you all enjoy. This will help you stay active, vital, fulfilled, and hopefully very happy.

Because you're making the effort to create a wonderful life, you might as well keep yourself healthy so you can enjoy it as long as possible!

I'm no health expert, but the good news is, to be healthy is pretty simple. It starts with a good healthy diet. You can do an online search for "healthy diet" and find all kinds of eating plans that you think you'll like. We all know we should eat plenty of vegetables and fruits. These days we can go to Walmart, get a cheap blender, and mix up all kinds of healthy drinks to give us the daily nutrients and proteins our body needs.

In addition to a good diet, we must MOVE. Yes, that means get off the couch, turn off the TV, put down the phone, and do something that gets our heart rate to where it needs to be for a period of time that's healthy.

You can do this by deciding which healthy activities you enjoy, or can tolerate, and figure out ways to do them on a regular basis. To make it more enjoyable, listen to music or a podcast, watch a video as you're exercising, or look around if you're moving your body outside in beautiful places.

We must also get plenty of sleep so when we're awake we're rested and feel better.

I used to look at my phone to "relax" before I went to bed. That was anything but relaxing because I always stayed up a lot later than planned, and the blue light of the phone wasn't helping my eyes or melatonin level, which is the hormone that regulates our body's sleep and wake cycle.

Part of my schedule these days is getting to sleep at a regular time, without phone bingeing prior. I wake up much more refreshed and *happy*, ready to take on the important activities first thing in the morning so I can spend the rest of the day doing things I enjoy with the people and animals that mean the most to me.

Now it's time to create *your* HEALTHY and HAPPY LIFE! That way when YOU are happy, those around you will be happy because they are with YOU!

The bottom line is please take care of yourself because you're creating an amazing life here and I want you to be able to enjoy it for as long as possible…and YOU ARE WORTH IT!

I will share more fun ways to help us both continue to be healthy and wealthy in my newsletter and podcast.

LET'S MAKE A DEAL TOGETHER

You and I began this book's journey together in the introduction where I shared the promise I made to myself while sitting in my mobile home back in the 1990's. That promise was that if I were ever to find a solution to my money prayers, that I would share it with others who were hoping and praying for someone to help them with their money challenges as well.

If you're now feeling a sense of Hope, Enthusiasm, and Excitement about your financial future from this moment forward, we are well on our way.

I'd like to start making good on MY NEXT PROMISE TO YOU...

I promise to provide you with NEW passive income sources to consider adding to your Stack, up and above what you'll find in this book, on a daily basis inside my FREE "Extra Income Sources" online newsletter starting RIGHT NOW. Please see what I have waiting for you now Absolutely Free... **PassiveIncomeStacking.com/start-here**

I also promise to share more exciting details on money generating solutions with you on "The Passive Income Stacking Show" podcast found here...

PassiveIncomeStacking.com

All you need to do now is sign up for my free "Extra Income Sources" newsletter.

Do we have a deal?

Good...I can't wait to share more with YOU online starting TODAY!

ONE LAST MONEY STORY

This is just the beginning! As soon as you become a subscriber to my free newsletter, I hope our time together will continue online for years to come like with so many of my subscribers.

Now, to wrap up the starting point of our journey together here, please allow me to share this story with you…

My first memory of money was when I was 4 years old living in Fresno, California in 1967. Summers there were very hot and the music calling from the ice cream truck was always a welcome sound.

Every once in a while as a special treat, my mother would kindly give me a dime to hand to the ice cream man to buy a popsicle. Yes, that's how much they cost back then.

From that day forward, I thought the person on the dime was the ice cream man!

With that in mind, I hope this book provides you with many ways to bring Financial Security and Happiness to your life, and enough dimes in your pocket to keep you smiling each time you hear the ice cream truck coming :-)

Your Friend,

Mark

P.S. If you found this book helpful, would you please kindly post an honest comment about it online so together we can help even more people who really need it right now. Thank you!

RESOURCES

FREE "EXTRA INCOME SOURCES" NEWSLETTER

This book is NOT static. It's merely the starting point of our journey and friendship together. Every day I share all kinds of passive income sources to consider with my loyal newsletter subscribers. I've been sending it out for decades and it's absolutely free…

Want even MORE Passive Income Sources to consider? Don't miss another day of my **FREE Daily "Extra Income Sources" Online News-letter** where I share NEW ways to generate Passive Income to better grow your Stack. **As a FREE BONUS you will also receive the "Passive In-come Stacking™ Quick Start Checklist" so you know how to begin with the most IMPACT!**

Subscribe for free at this link:

PassiveIncomeStacking.com/start-here

"THE PASSIVE INCOME STACKING SHOW" PODCAST

While you're driving, working out, doing chores, or just in need of some inspiration, be sure to listen to **"The Passive Income Stacking Show" podcast** episodes. Get ready to ROCK as we explore new income sources to consider adding to your Stack. There you'll also hear me interview Passive Income Giants as they share their unique income secrets.

Listen in and join the "Stacker Nation" at this link:

PassiveIncomeStacking.com/podcast

MY FREE ONLINE PASSIVE INCOME SCHOOL...

For years I've heard the financial horror stories about the growing epidemic of student loan debt. People go to college in good faith with the hopeful expectation that they'll graduate with the ability to earn a nice income. Sadly, many come out of school realizing their income will be far less than expected. To add insult to injury, they're often strapped with tens of thousands of dollars in student loans that will stay with them for decades.

This schooling crisis frustrated me so much that instead of continuing to get upset for all the people being hurt by it, I created a FREE SOLUTION...

Centered around the Passive Income Stacking™ "money generating model" that you'll learn in this book, I created a FREE online school where I continue to teach online classes that cover even more strategies and insights designed to help you MAKE MONEY and reach financial freedom FASTER regardless of your age or situation.

Everyone gets a FULL RIDE SCHOLARSHIP to my Passive Income School where the tuition is FREE because YOU are the VIP! Let's start doing this together right now – first learn the strategies in this book and then take advantage of the Free Passive Income Classes TODAY at…

PassiveIncomeSchool.VIP

WANT EVEN MORE PASSIVE INCOME SOURCES RIGHT NOW?

TM

That's my dog OTIS standing on <u>his</u> Stack. Because you've made it this far, you are now officially a member of "TEAM OTIS"! Are you getting excited about all the new and fun income sources that are ready for you to tap into at this very moment?

If you answered, "YES", you're in luck because I'm always updating my income sources page with new ideas for you to consider.

For a list of recently added income sources to consider adding to your Stack go to this link:

PassiveIncomeStacking.com/income-sources

ABOUT THE AUTHOR

Mark Walters is the President of PassiveIncomeSchool.VIP - CEO of CreatingWealthClub.com, LLC and PassiveIncomeStacking.com - a lover of God, family, friends, animals, music, fun, and a passionate entrepreneur. While struggling financially and sitting on $5 plastic chairs that were part of the hand-me-down table inside the "dining area" of his 1974, 12 foot by 60 foot single wide trailer where he lived for 6 years in the 1990's, he made himself this promise…

"If I ever figure out a way to raise myself up financially, I'm going to share the solution with others that are in this same type of situation, hoping and praying just like I'm doing right now".

Through his free online Passive Income School, free daily online "Extra Income Sources" newsletter, and free "The Passive Income Stacking Show" podcast, he's fulfilling the promise he made to himself decades prior by sharing money-generating solutions with those looking to raise themselves up financially.

SiT-O

PRODUCTIONS

NOTICE! The author and publisher of the material found here are not accountants or attorneys, and are not qualified nor are they giving any legal, accounting, or investing advice here or on their websites. Always consult a good attorney, accountant, financial planner, and estate planner BEFORE setting up the kind of things mentioned in this book and the websites listed.

All information is based on their research and is presented in good faith. They are not responsible for errors and omissions. No legal advice is being given in any of our material. Laws change from time to time. **Always consult an attorney before investing in real estate, or doing anything covered in this book, so you know you're doing things properly and lawfully in your area. No earnings claims are being made here. Results vary based on effort.** By reading this you understand this to be an expression of opinions and not professional advice. You are solely responsible for the use of any content and hold CreatingWealthClub.com, LLC and all members and affiliates harmless in any event or claim, demand, or damage, including reasonable attorneys' fees, asserted by any third party or arising out of your use of, or conduct on, this product and/or website/s.